HOW TO MAKE YOUR CHILD SMART AND INTELLIGENT?

A Practical Guidance for Parents

Dr. J.C. Lall & Dr. S.B. Lall

Notion Press

Old No. 38, New No. 6
McNichols Road, Chetpet
Chennai - 600 031

First Published by Notion Press 2018
Copyright © J.C. Lall & S.B. Lall 2018
All Rights Reserved.

ISBN 978-81-901850-7-3

DEDICATION

This book is dedicated to the parents who by their selfless efforts bring up
their children, to make them important members of the society.

Dr. J.C. Lall

MB, BS; M.D. (PAED), MAMS, C.F. (FR).

Senior Consultant Child Specialist

Formerly Child specialist PGI, Chandigarh,

Asst. Professor of Paediatrics,

Post-Graduate Institute of Medical

Education & Research, Rohtak

Professor Paediatrics Artemis Health Institute, Gurgaon

Visiting Pediatrician BLK Super Specialty Hospital, New Delhi

Dr. S.B. Lall

MB, BS; MD., DGO, MNAMS, FAMS

Formerly Additional Professor

All India Institute of Medical Sciences, New Delhi

Specialist-Environmental Health

Ministry of Health – Sultanate of Oman

2018

1st Edition

**PEOPLE HEALTH SERIES
PUBLICATION**

Important

Always consult your doctor before taking any treatment. This book is a supplement to understanding of the subject "Making your child smart and intelligent"

1st Edition 2018

PEOPLE HEALTH SERIES PUBLICATION

F-152 Mansarover Garden, New Delhi-110015 INDIA

Telephone: 091–11–25938526

Mobile: 091–9811106043, 0091–9911106043

Fax: 091–11–45640327

Email: jclall2002@yahoo. com,

jclall2002@gmail. com

Website: www. childmother. com

Medical Editor: Dr. S.B. Lall

Consultant Editor: Dr. J.C. Lall

1st Edition 2018

Printed in INDIA

A Message

The child is a gift of life. It is the duty of parents to bring up the child with enthusiasm, provide them best care and education. No child should be left uncared for, in this world. Intelligence illuminates the body, soul and mind.

Contents

Preface

We all are human beings, born in similar manner but those who are brought up in a careful way, make the difference for good, become the real winners. Since, early years of childhood are most important when a young ignited mind could be molded towards betterment.

This book will help the parents about stimulation of child's mind to learn and grow and not about the routine body requirements of feeding, clothing or dealing with particular diseases. Most important as parents, we should help our children to understand the world around them but the parents often spend their time with the child worrying about their feeding, toilet training and their get ups. They do not know that a young developing child's brain needs to be taken care of. The child in his early life is eager to learn and exploring the world with budding intelligence and can be molded easily for learning. This book is a guide to methods by which the child can be taught during early years in his own style and correct speed to make him smart and intelligent.

Initially the emotional and intellectual development of child takes place during first six years of life, when the parents can raise the child's smartness and intelligence level substantially by taking good care of him.

In the past, it was presumed that the child will develop according to his own growth time table but researches have shown that it is not entirely so. Some change in the environment can make lot of life-long difference in child's mental development. At home, parents being closest to the child and are first and influential teachers who can influence the child's environment. Our aim in this book is to make the child intelligent, may it be book smarter or environmental smarter. Both of these are important in real life.

Though the children differ from one another, so their parents, home and circumstances do. Every child has his own characteristic and the emotions. He may get them from his mother during pregnancy and his potentials are also different. Parents must consider the emotion and potentials of the child while raising his or her. The transactional nature of child development ensures that child's status at any single point of time can never predict the later development.

For younger children, the stronger single prediction for later development is child's environment. This book will suggest the parents, some ideas about helping the growing minds of their children and enable them to perceive the difference in growth pattern. We are grateful to our colleague physicians, psychiatrists, educationist and psychologists who tirelessly helped us by giving their suggestions and comments.

Instead of writing he or she and avoiding repetition, we have used the word 'child.' This book is expected to be useful for parents in general living any where in the world.

Why Should You Raise a Smart and Intelligent Child

01

1. 1. Aim of the family

In several parts of the world it is assumed that children are born and brought up to serve the aims of the family. As they grow up, they prepare themselves for the work at jobs as considered suitable for family. They are also expected to marry in an arranged way by parents for the purpose of advancing the family. For these purposes smartness and intelligence counts most.

1. 2. Family expectation

At many places, the parents have been in agreement that children should serve their own country. The children are encouraged to be dedicated to their country. They should be studious, smart and co-operative so that the parents may not keep worrying about them and the children should grow up happier and stable to serve humanity which is the purpose of being human.

1. 3. Need of idealistic children

If the child is an idealistic one, he will have all the opportunities present in the country. We do have wrong doing in our races, such as divorces, suicide, crime which are disgrace to our community. Few children do not take the responsibility of the family and indulge in alcoholism and smoking and avoid working. Such practices could be avoided if the children are idealistic and co-operative. We should bring up our children with a feeling that we have been brought in this world to serve others and not just for their own satisfaction. The child should be taught to respect their parents and shall not be allowed to call bad names, bite or pull the hair of their parents. We should teach our children a smart and cooperative way of life. By two years of age the child should be taught to pick up his own toys, play and keep them back at proper places. By three years, the child should be encouraged to dump the waste in waste-basket and help in small chores such as helping the parents in laying table which would give them a feel of cooperation though it would not save their time. At seven or eight years of age, other small tasks could be done by the child such as bringing small things from adjacent shops. As adolescents, they have lot more to play the role in studies, community and society service. They should be able to feel concern for their parents and helping to solve family problems. The children at school should be able to get along with each other and should be able to analyse the problems of their future chosen fields. They should be prepared to work as volunteer in school and serve the society.

1. 4. Raising the child in stressful society

As the industrialization and cost of living are increasing, the competition is also increasing. The parents transmit their excessive competitiveness to their children and try to teach the curriculum to them even at less than 2 years of age to make them "super children" in a short time. Such a child does not understand the meaning of all that and avoids such education, thereby the anxiety level of the parent increase leading to stress and quarrelsome atmosphere in the family. Both the parents usually work outside and find less time to look after their small children, by which children are deprived of their parental care and parents feel guilty about it.

Stress is also felt by women for their discrimination in pay and prestige in their goals to make both ends meet and also do not find any creative satisfaction. Racial discrimination is disturbingly high. Drugs and alcohol abuse is on the rise which causes family stress.

The life is becoming materialistic and the spiritualization is on the decrease, thus society is becoming stressful. In such a stressful society, we must make our children co-operative, loved to respect people, feeling and careful for family and social activity. School also plays its role in reformation of children. The violence in TV and cinema should also be curbed. Family atmosphere plays a great role in transformation of children.

1. 5. Can we make a child brighter

After many experimentation and researches, it has been discovered that even a child of two years can be taught to read and even one year old can be taught to recognize the various pictures. If we give right mental stimulus to a small child at home and school he can be made to a brighter child for his distinguished carrier later on. With this we do not mean that child should be burdened by a curriculum. On the contrary if the child is neglected or consistently ignored, his mind and spirit fails to develop fully. Now the question is what is mental stimulation? A normal child is an born explorer and wants to reach people and the things and wants to respond to other. If the parents respondfavourably to his habit of discovery, smiling, showing love with hugs and comforting him during misery, offering food and water at the time of requirement, keeping the child for passing waste. Such gestures make the foundation stimuli for the child on which the future relationship of child-parent develop. His school performance also develops on this foundation of such love and trust. Such children develop their vocabulary fast and become intensely curious about everything they see or hear and tend to mature emotionally and intellectually fast in this pattern themselves. The goal of their future development is emotional, social and intellectual development which shall be better than the other children.

Such natural interplay between children and parents produce plenty of loving, capable and bright children. For a small child, any special equipment for such development is not required. Such a parental behavior makes the child to develop interest and initiative that make them robot in their own fields in future and hero in the family. Children should be brought up and appreciated and loved for their whole person and not just fast for their looks or musculature, though such special gifts may also be appreciated.

How Does the Brain Work?

2. 1. The brain

The brain is soft structure and works as control centre of the body. It is situated inside the skull box. It contains around 100 billion nerve cells, almost equivalent to number of stars in our galaxy. It consists of two hemispheres connected to each other. The surface of brain is folded and looks like walnut. These are called cerebral hemispheres. Each hemisphere is made of different areas which take different functions of the body. There is another part at the back under the hemisphere which is called cerebellum which control the body balance, posture and coordination of movement. The hemispheres have outer layer (grey matter) called cortex and consists of nerve cells and is arbitrarily divided into different lobes, frontal, parietal, temporal, and posterior (occipipal). This is useful for difficult mental tasks, control of movement, sensory perception and speech. The inner layer is white matter and contains nerve fibres (axons) to carry signals across the body. The two hemisphere are connected to each other as well as midbrain, pons, medulla and spinal cord. The spinal cord lies in vertebral column, and is connected with body organs by nerves. Frontal part of the brain is responsible for personality, emotions and social behaviour. Grey matter of parietal lobe in centre is responsible for most difficult tasks (calculation, language, movements, some sensations) and orders the muscle group of hands and feet or other part to carry out functions. While temporal lobes on the sides deals with language, memory and sensation of hearing and smell and posteriors lobes with vision.

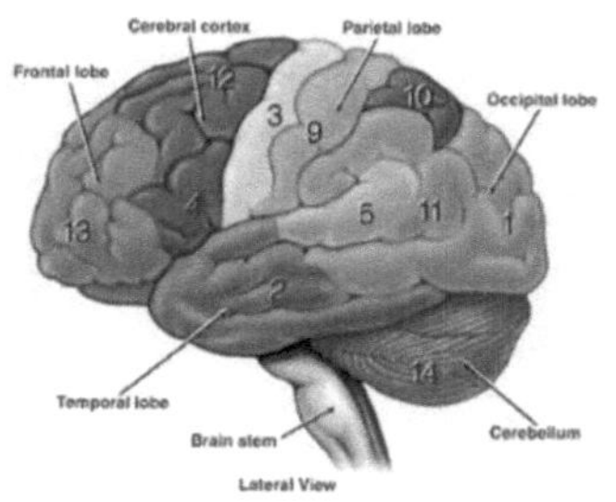

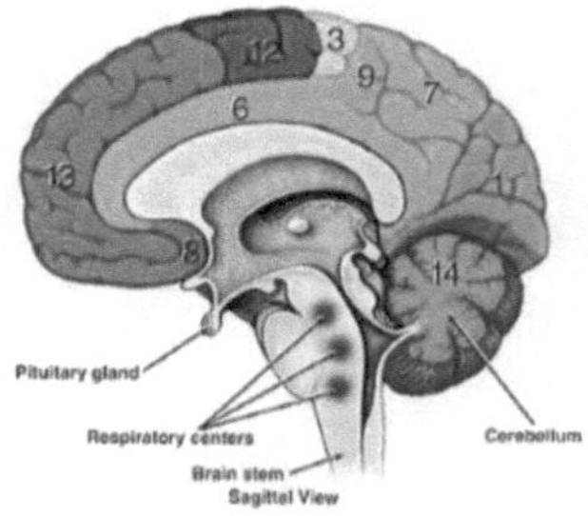

Whole Brain   **Section of Brain**

Grey and white matter

The grey part of your brain is the outer layer or cortex. You use it for the most difficult mental tasks, the reason it looks grey is because it consists mainly of nerve cells. The while matter is the inner layer that is made from nerve fibres, or axons. These carry signals across the brain.

What does your brain look like?

The surface of your brain, or cortex, is folded and looks like a large walnut, or a small cauliflower. It is divided into two halves, known as cerebral hemispheres, which are connected to each other. Each cerebral hemisphere is made up of several different lobes, which are named after skull bones covering them. The cortex is crinkly because its millions of little folds increase the surface area.

2. 2. Processing information

The electrical signals from the body and around reach the brain in millions. These signals carry information to the brain. The brain processes them and decides the usefulness of these signals. Some of these signals carry information about body movement and body function while others are for generating ideas and making decisions. The hardest job of the brain is to understand them. Still we have to know about brain's working. As the signals are received in the brain, they are processed and some sense is made out of information and the brain orders the body parts such as upper and lower limbs, eyes, ears, mouth to work to response to the signals. Both halves of the brain have important functions. The senses such as sight, hearing, smell and taste are control by the same side of hemisphere while movement and skin perception are controlled by opposite hemisphere through nerves.

2. 3. Learning and memory

Think of learning a new thing. The child may require to practice the task ones, twice or many times. Every time, the child is using his past experience to help it out, if one does not practice, he is likely to remember only a part of the job. But catching up a quicker each time. Once the child has mastered it, the brain remembers the skill and stores it as memory. This how the learning is acquired.

Focusing the task

You will remember more, and learn faster, if you are working towards a goal, such as passing a test or receiving a reward. The more you concentrate on your task, the quicker you will learn and remember. It also helps if you enjoy the task and you receive praise for your effort.

Keeping healthy brain

Stimulating the mind- Although short – term memory ability declines as you get older, you can carry on learning new skills at any age. To learn, you need to keep an active mind. Reading, conversation, visiting new places, and playing games (even some computer games) are all stimulating for the mind.

The child learns either by his inquisitiveness or by associating one thing with other or learns by being told about it using all the senses. He/She remembers the thing by focusing at the task. The focusing or concentration at the task he develops by passing the test by praise or receiving the awards for the task. He will not concentrate or focus if the atmosphere around him, is not congenial such as fears, anxiety or negativity exists which will make learning difficult. He will learn quicker if he enjoys the task. One cannot remember everything. The brain stores only the portion of memories.

2. 4. How does the memory work?

There are two different types of memories, The Short term memory is what has just been told such as recent events or phone numbers or what you had in lunch. It has a limited capacity and only lasts for short time. The other is long term memory such as cycling, driving etc.

The brain has amazing long term memory storing capacity which stays for long, may be forever. A lot of learning and creativity occurs through experimentation, by trying different ideas such as music composition, computer programming etc.

2. 5. Stimulating the brain

Although short term memory ability declines as the child gets older but carrying out new skills by brain stimulation, the task can be learnt better at early age. To learn, the child has to be of active mind which can be made by stimulation such as reading, conversation, visiting new places and playing games (computer games, dance, drama, music, chess and outdoor and indoor games). All of these stimulate the mind.

2. 6. What happens when the child is deprived of brain stimulation?

The children who are deprived of normal stimuli if continued, shall suffer from mental changes, hearing and visual hallucination, anxiety, depression and insanity. Low stimulation is produced if a child is kept in a unit and remains unattended and uncared for a long time where the problems may be of less magnitude. In severe case, if child is kept in small sound-proof room for a longer time where there is darkness and sound, does not reach over these, the problems are of large extent, that will make the child mad.

2. 7. Wisdom and intelligence

Wisdom is intelligence shaped by experience. It is a complex state of thought process and is not easy to describe. It is the ability to make sound choice and good decision and is characterized by profound understanding and deep insight but is not necessarily accompanied by extensive formal education. Wise person can be found in various walks of life such as carpenters, fishermen, housewives and many more and is not confined to specialized field or discipline. A wise person is aware of wholeness and is conscious of integrity and is able to make correct judgement and decisions. It is intangible quality of a person gained through experience from culture philosophy of religion and comes from pure reasoning while others believe that it comes from intuition and spirituality.

2. 8. Good sleep for good memory

A good night's sleep not only leaves child feeling refreshed it could also improve child' memory, according to researchers at America's Boston University Medical School.

The US study investigated the role of sleep in a process called memory consolidation when memories caused by new activities and information are solidified in the brain. Tests showed that this process is more efficient after a full night's sleep.

Lead researcher Dr. Matthew Walker said: "When you are asleep it seems that you are shifting memory to more efficient storage regions within the brain."

"Consequently, when you wake up, memory tasks can be performed far more quickly and accurately with less stress and anxiety." Dr. Walker said the findings might explain that children and teenagers need more sleep than adults and why babies sleep almost round the clock.

Sleep

Sleep has restorative functions and is important for conservation of energy and growth. It comprises of two distinct states, rapid eye movement (REM) sleep and non rapid eye movement (non REM), occurring in cycles one after another during the sleep. Non-REM gives light and deep sleep, night terrors and sleepwalking while REM is responsible for anxiety dreams, nightmares. The cycle is about 50–60 min in children as compared to adult which around 90 min.

2. 9. Sleep requirement

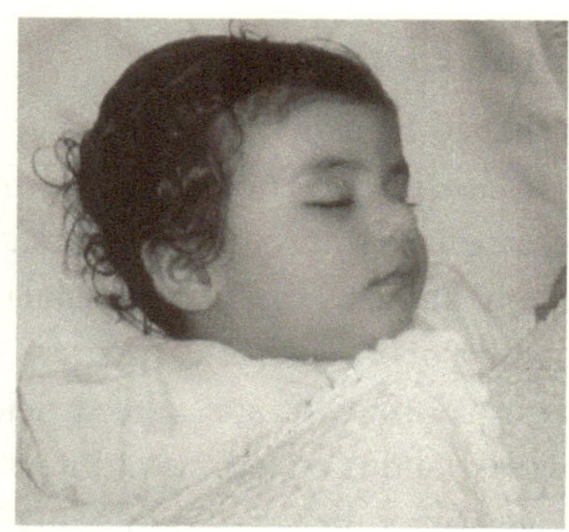

Sleep

The sleep alternates between period of wakefulness. In 2 to 6 months old child, the sleep requirement is approximately 14–16 hours per day and by age of six months, it is about 9–11 hours at night and 3 hours during daytime. A child of 1–2 years sleeps around 13–14 hours per day with night sleep of 8–12 hours and the sleep is more sound. At 2–5 years of age the sleep is about 11–13 hours per day. The following table shows the sleep requirement in children.

Age	Sleep hrs. per day (24 hours)	Night sleeping hrs/day	Day naps hrs/day
1 week	16	8–9	7–8
1 month	15	8–9	6–7
6 month	14	11	3
12 month	14	12	2
18 month	13	12	1
2 year	13	12	1
5 year	11	11	-
8–10 year	9–10	9–10	-
12–15 year	8–9	8–9	-
18 year	8	8	-

When the child is around three years of age or more, he may resist afternoon sleep. The sleep is considered adequate when after sleeping, the child gets up fresh, is playful, non – irritable and also eating well.

2. 10. Problems caused by sleeplessness

Some children struggle around bedtime and show difficulty in establishing regular night sleep. Such children may show general fussiness and irritability. In an infant, the lack of sleep may be due to hunger, pain, over clothing/under clothing, unsuitable environment, nasal block or illness.

The sleep disorders may be due to parental anxiety. Older children sometimes have fears (burglars, noises, lightening, thunder etc), which interfere in sleep. They even may delay bedtime and/or try to sleep in parents bedroom. Separation anxiety often contributes to problem of sleeplessness and the child considers sleep as the time of removal from the parents. Family conflicts or normal separation such as going to school also contributes towards sleeplessness. Other anxiety like fear of death, school performances or depression can also cause sleeplessness. Few children may suffer from nightmares, night terrors and sleepwalking.

What Is Intelligence?

Every society and culture has a word "smart," "clever," "intellectual," "brainy," "achiever," "brilliant," "bright," "gifted" or "stupid," "dull," "slow" and so on which is valued by our society is the test measure for our intelligence. It is always a debatable point as to what is intelligence? Psychologist look intelligence as biological process while ecologist focus it on environmental basis. Both of them do not concede each other. However, intelligence has been defined as ability for complex thinking and reasoning which requires mental activity. The expert emphasizes that ability to learn from experience and ability to adopt to once environment is included in intelligence. Ability to engage in abstract thinking, general adaptability to new problems in life, capacity for acquiring knowledge and knowledge possessed, general capacity for independence, originality and productiveness in thinking, capacity to acquire relevant relationship, ability to judge, to understand and to reason out and general cognitive ability, are included in intelligence.

3. 1. IQ intelligence

Intelligence is measure by testing intelligence quotient (IQ) of a child. It is the most widely used for intelligence which indicates mental ability relative to others. In a small child of 4 weeks to 5 years of age, we use development quotient. People in general population conceive intelligence, as cleverness, commonsense, communication ability safety, self-care, self direction, health, practical problem solving ability, verbal ability and interest in learning skills along with social competence and work are the components of intelligence.

3. 2. Calculation of IQ (Intelligence Quotient)

First intelligence test used by Binet – Simon in 1905 in France for children who move behind in academic. The measurement of intelligence is made by intelligence quotient (IQ) which was introduced by a French psychologist, Alfred Binet, in the beginning of twentieth century was modified by Terman as the way to place the kids within IQ system. The child is tested for his verbally and his activity. The IQ is calculated as follows:

$$\frac{mental\,age}{chronological\,age} \times 100 = IQ$$

It is depicted in points. Each test is designed specifically for a particular age range of children with verbal and performance. At the age of three years, the kids are given 20 pictures and related 20 questions based on them. At 4–6 years of age child is tested for pictures, words and 25 related questions and numbers. The test takes about 40 minutes to complete. For kids of 7–9 years 35 multiple choice question about numbers, series, words and pictures are included which takes about 60 minutes and children of about 10–15 years of age are asked for 40 multiple choice question focusing on numbers series, words, pictures and mathematical skills. In 1925 Gesell developmental schedule was used to measure development quotient (DQ) for children age 4 weeks to 5 years. In DQ, gross motor skill, fine motor skill, language, adaptive behaviour and social behaviour was tested. Such test are used for identification of child intellectual capability, abstract thinking, logical, mathematical skills, visual – spatial capability, linguistic physical activity and perceptual aptitude test but not measuring all other types of intelligence such at emotional and social. Mental age levels off round as the end of adolescent age. It is difficult to convert IQ for achievements and ability. Stanfod – Binet – Wechster (WISE III test is widely used these days).

Though there are several tests for mental screening of the child. An acceptable test must be sensitive and reasonably specific and should measure similar results on repeat administration. It should be relatively quick and inexpensive. None of the test is entirely satisfactory. DDST (Denver Developmental Screening Test) is widely used which provides four domains such as personal, social, fine motor adaptive, language and gross motor skills for children from birth to six years. It can be administered in 20–30 minutes without extensive training or expensive equipment DDST – II as greatly expanded language section and has greater sensitivity. The test identifies the delays in development.

3. 3. IQ test score interpretation

IQ is depicted in scores which tells how bright a child is compared to other. The average IQ of our half population is 90–110, while 25% have higher IQ and 25% have lower. The average IQ by definition is taken 90–110. The score above 110 indicate higher than average and below 90 indicates below average. In practice, the maximum upper limit is 150. Hence, over 140 score (0.5% population) is considered genius and 130 + scores (2.5% population) are considered very superior, 120–129 superior, 110–119 high average, 90–109 average, 80–89 low average, 70–79 border line and below 70 extremely low. IQ of 40–55 is trainable group and below this are severe (IQ 25–40)and profound retardation means IQ< 20–25. Mental retardation (2.5% population). IQ of Albert Einstein a scientist was judged to be 160.

3. 4. Prediction of future carrier on the basis of IQ

Measurement of intelligence may be valuable but values may be overrated. The classification given below is arbitrary. No one should be either alarmed or discouraged if he found IQ of the child not high upto expectation. Many elements besides IQ contribute to success and happiness. Child's IQ test score may be used to help predict career or job that the child would be suited for, though child may prefer to choose another job as an adult. Generally IQ test score are thought to relate following profession which may have small correlation.

IQ Score	Profession
90 -	Gardner, farmland, miner, packer, sorter
90–100	Custodian, factory workers, labourer, cook, baker, small farmer.
100–110	File clerk, truck driver, shipping clerk, telephone operator, carpenter, mail clerk, machine operator, welder
110–120	Account clerk, sales representative, electrician, plumber, book keeper, policeman
120–130	Service manager, Administrator, Engineer, Computer Specialist, Estate Agent, Pharmacist, Nurses, School teacher.
130 and above	Professor, Scientist, Lawyer, Doctor, Engineer.
140 -	Civil servant, Research Scientist

The IQ of the child can be raised if the child is cared for at an early age

3. 5. Smartness

Smartness in general terms is considered to be a child who is physically and mentally clever, uses his wisdom in all tasks, lively and witty. Such children are quick to progress in our society and such children understand the outcome of the task much earlier than a common child and are society excellent in behaviour.

Human intelligence, we often understand by school intelligence that is book smart children. **But according to experts intelligence is broadly categorized into two types – environmental smartness (street smart) and book smart. The book smart children are good at books and hardly know anything beyond books. On the other hand, environmental (street smart) children are the those who can easily gauze the environment to deal with the situation which is often not found in the books which is the demand of today's world.**

We often hear the stories that a classmate or neighbors have their maturity beyond their educational capability. Such children have often been mediocre or last in the class bunking their classes. They never had answers to oral tests but have biggest circle of friends. They some how manage to pass the examination in low grade. When their classmates are busy in acquiring higher education, these children are busy helping their parents in business. By the time their classmates acquire university grade, these street smart children establish a good business. **There is no doubt that such children have picked up book knowledge to make their environmental wisdom strong but are not book worms.** They use their skills such as shrewdness and astuteness an effective tools to handle the world.

On the other hand book smart children are smart with the books only and learn lot from books but know little beyond them. Such children score high in examination but may have problems in making connection between book knowledge and life situation. When things around them change, they hardly realize them, that is, they want to enter the station when train had already left. This is just opposite to street smartness.

To give example, if we imagine that in a dark street with bad neighbourhood, two dangerous looking persons are roaming around looking to make trouble. A book smart person might not be aware enough to notice the situation and might walk towards them and end up by getting hits from them. But a street smart, on the other hand would be aware of the environment and would be able to judge the dangerous person and would avoid them. Obviously, a street smart child is having the ability to learn things from life and experience and has good judgement on life situations at crucial moments such as in emergency and serious dangers.

Our educational system has often focused on scores in examination and is producing a lot of books smarts, but how they are going to live in this world that require street smart children. Only theory hardly works when you have to be practical to meet your ends. The book smart children take their time, generally slow but eliminate error by knowing expected results and take long to become successful.

But there are intelligent, sophisticated, verbal and successful street smart types as well who becoming adult, run companies, offices and teach in major universities and received awards for competence. Hence we feel that mixture of both street smartness and book smartness is important in life. Only book smart most often tend to take a second slot after the street smart.

Elements of both types of smartness is necessary for good foundation to success – academics as well as environmental and emotional. It is believed that street smartness is acquired through media, influences from the people and personal experience in coping with ups and downs of life.

It is important for children to be street smart as well because the surrounding of the children are very challenging and demanding for their own situations. **Street smartness is demanded when interacting with other people and for introspection. Book smartness is demanded in academically challenging situations. However, in every situation, these two interact in a logical thinking.**

Both street and book smarts children will succeed in life but street smart children will be two or three steps ahead in later life. Hence to achieve a perfect blend of book smartness and street smartness, a child needs to attempt all-rounder individual. One cannot be educated solely on what one reads or solely on what one lives with, hence one needs a combination of the two. Our activities and problems in our daily life require use of common sense just not solely based on books but actual experience which requires mixture of book and environmental knowledge. Although education can make one powerful and in some rich but there is more life than that. Being street smart you are sensitive to environment and quick to adapt the situations. A formal education appears to be less important without knowledge of society that surrounds us.

What Is the Basis of Making the Child Brighter | 04

Many researches have made in the field of medicine, education and psychology including behavioural science regarding the ability of learning of children at various age groups and have found that children of various types of backgrounds can learn more and can become more intelligent.

Such researches are still on to verify above statement regarding involving the children from various social, economic and educational, genetic, city or village background for long time, which have put the parents in new direction to rearing of children.

The following facts were noted. The concept shall be better understood by following theories.

4. 1. Child's intelligence in changeable

It was initially thought that every child had predetermined intellectual growth which could reach to a specific level in his life but it is not true. The child does not have fixed level of intelligence, it is changeable to better or worse by his environment during early years of life.

The intelligence is measured by intelligence quotient (IQ) test. The normal values of IQ were considered to be between 90–110. It is true that for majority of school children, IQ seems to stay relatively constant and score of some children vary tremendously before school years.

In one research IQ of 152 children was repeatedly tested between the ages of twenty one months to eight years of age. In two children it was found to be risen by more than 70 points. This difference separates these children as gifted from general children. The changes were much seen in many children between 30–50 points. It does not mean that it only rises it may decrease as well depending upon the stimulus given and the family atmosphere but usually 15 percent maintain the ten points variations even in school years. Researches also show that there is small relationship between 2 and 5 years of age.

It is considered that IQ changes because of change in child's intelligence. The increase and decrease in IQ is caused by positive stimulation or lack of it in the environment. For example if a child is put in orphanage where he hardly gets mental stimulation, he is likely to become mentally dull around a period of three months. If he is further deprived of mental stimulation, he would further decline in his intelligence. Mothers do give lot of care to children and in their absence the child gets less mental stimulation. This type of retardation is due to maternal deprivation.

In another experiment, few children were admitted in an orphanage when they were less than one month of age and were kept in an individual cribs with soft mattresses where they laid on their back. On the soft mattress, the child will sag and it is difficult for him to turn the side. The children were fed by propped up bottles and had not been given toys. They were given bath every day and were changed whenever necessary by the attendants. Though the room was kept clean but children did not get any other mental stimulation. When children learnt to sit up, they were made to sit on floor during waking hours. Around the age of two years, even less than half of the children could sit up and none could walk, being otherwise normal physically. They were compared to other non instutionalized children at that age who were walking easily. At three years of age orphanage children could sit up themselves and only 15% could walk.

Yet another experience in Iran, few children were admitted to orphanage where there was more contact with attendants. They were held in lap while feeding and were propped up in sitting position and were given few toys to play with. There growth was considered as normal when compared with non instutionalized children. More of them at one year could sit alone, and at two years could walk holding to hands or chair.

This shows that even a little added mental stimulation could produce great gains in development of children.

Another study showed that children between seven months to one year of age admitted to orphanage who were unable to sit, were exposed to stimulation and were allowed to handle various objects such as papers bags, coloured sponges, plastic toys, boxes, coloured plastic dishes, flowers, few small bottles, metal ash trays etc. just for one hour a day. The children were propped up in low chairor on the floor. Even without the help of adults, these children learnt to sit up independently and took interest in playing. **The development was fourtime faster as compared to non stimulated children. This shows beyond doubt that child's intelligence can be changed, it increases if mental stimulation is given and it could lower if no stimulation was given in early life. That** means if you enrich the child environment with mental stimulation, you can always increase his intelligence. Mental stimulation, we mean by loving, cuddling, kissing, playing, talking, feeding and taking care of daily needs of the child early in life. Such children are likely to be brighter later in life. This is what behavioural scientists are spreading their message to the parents.

Their various experiments show that it is feasible to raise average level of intelligence by about 30 points. This is a welcome message to the general population that intelligence was previously consider a fixed quality and is better understood now as changeable and experimentation is still going on to find better ways of intelligence boosting techniques.

4. 2. Mental capacity is greatest when brain is growing rapidly

The child's brain is fast growing up to age of 6–8 years, when the child is younger, the environmental affect is the maximum on his growing brain including level of intelligence. So the stimuli, the child gets during this stage will have long lasting effects on his brain.

More mental stimuli means better intelligence, lack of stimuli means dullness in a particular child. The same amount of mental stimuli given to a high school child or during elementary years will not result in that large gains.

The researches numbering, more than thousand, have shown that the intelligence is changing most rapidly during first 6–8 years of life. After this age, the intellectual development does not proceed at uniform rate but is at decreasing rate which can not be made up in later years. The future learning will depend upon past experience. A child who had started enjoying his studies will be far different than other children of his classes.

Dark and crowded flats, having no books and few toys where the mothers are much preoccupied and cannot give their time to children, cause great loss of intelligence in such children when compared with better home environment.

Dr. Bloom writes that what a child learns early in life has powerful impact on his brain which is persistent and it differs from late learning in its effectiveness. Hence early years are vital in child care.

During early years of rapid learning, an environmental lacking or abundant in mental stimuli can change a child's IQ as much as 20–30 points according to Dr. Bloom. This can affect the professional career and occupation whether the child will be a skilled, semiskilled or an unskilled person in later life.

Thus we can dramatically reduce the incidence of low levels of intelligence and increase proportion of individuals of better or higher intelligence which will affect the country's progress as whole.

4. 3. Role of heredity

Many researchers have undertaken to answer the question of effect of nature versus environment over child intelligence. Since both factors are so complex that no one can control them to answer and it is virtually impossible to separate them. Certain children do very well in schools because their fathers and mothers are educated and intelligent or because their children remain attached to have atmosphere where book reading and learning is practiced by the parents.

Heridity may be putting an upper limit on your child's intelligence capacity but it may be 65–70 percent.

It is agreed that the basic quality of brain in children may be inherited by genes of their parents. These genes may be for special talent in the child such as music, mathematical skills which can be traced in generations but child's environmental mental stimuli determine rest of the chores by mental development. It determines how quickly the child can learn from the environment.

The basic qualities of the genetic configuration cannot be changed in the child, he may be one with strong body but poor quality of brain or vice versa or of a mixes constitution, but you can certainly change the child's environment in many ways which will affect the development of his inherited potentials just like just you can develop his physique.

The brain has tremendous power and potential of development of intellect that no one has fully achieved so far. It has been studied that two biological sibs brought up by two separate middle class families when separated and remain out of their own, their IQ became similar. The reason may be that they were free to let their genotype express themselves and they were not dictated by their parents.

4. 4. Intelligence is not influenced by birth order

It was initially thought that first born child is the family is smarter and likely to become leaders in later life, however this belief is not true. It was thought that large families make low IQ children but it may be influenced by low IQ parents who make large families. Smart people tend to have small families. There has been no casual role of family size in determination of child's IQ according to researches.

4. 5. IQ may be related to breastfeeding

Many researches have undertaken to know the influence of breastfeeding in children.

It is generally considered that the breast fed children grew with higher IQ than other sibs in the family who were not given breastfeed.

It may be due to environmental influences at that amount of time that mother and child spend together during breastfeeding and sense of closeness from nursing which stimulate the child's brain.

After controlling such factors, researches have found out that the breastfed children gain IQ by 3 to 8 points by age of 3 years, which may be because of immunity against the diseases, provided by breast milk. The child gains the energy as breast milk being rich source of omega – 3 fatty acids, that builds block of nerve cells membrane of the brain which effects-transmission of nerve impulses to help raising IQ.

4. 6. Effect of diet on IQ

Recent studies confirm our parents wisdom that diet influences brain functioning. They say, eat your fish, it is a brain food.

Researchers in New York City school examined IQ of approximately one million children and found that when preservative, dyes, colours and artificial flavours were removed from lunch diet, there was 14 percent improvement in children's IQ and improvement was greatest in weakest students.

All such material in diet has deleterious effect on brain cells functioning, thus decrease IQ.

4. 7. IQ is correlated to head size

Scholars from nineteenth century tried to establish the correlation between head size contour and the brain. Neuro-imaging technique in science have demonstrated that a head volume is in correlation with IQ, however the correlation is quite small.

4. 8. IQ is on the rise

Jame Fyan compared the IQ of today's children with the grandparents performance of 50 years ago. He found that IQ of present generation has risen approximately by 20 points.

The rise in IQ has been attributed to many factors such as more schooling, better environment, good nutrition and better educated parents, smart toys, computers and TV programmes.

4. 9. IQ scores have predictive Value

The topic have already been discussed (3. 4)

4. 10. IQ versus school attendance

Many studies have been undertaken and it has been observed that staying in school itself can elevate IQ and with each additional month a student remaining in school may increase his IQ above, what would have been expected, had he dropped out. South Africa researchers are of the expression that for each year of delayed schooling, children experience a decrement of IQ by 5 points.

Similar studies have been made in US also. Two independent studies have documented that there is systematic decline in IQ scores over summer vacations.

4. 11. Intelligence in plural and not singular

Robert Stenberg a psychologist in 1995 demonstrated that practical and analytical intelligence are two different things. He observed that skills of practical intelligence such as common sense were important in predicting life outcome but were not associated with IQ type of analytical intelligence. Howard Gardner of Harvard was of opinion there were at least seven or eight different kinds of intelligence such as intrapersonal, interpersonal, linguistic, motoric and musical intelligence.

Expert in particular field are better in reasoning than non-experts regardless of IQ scores.

Different types of intelligences

French Psychologists Alfred Binet developed means of determining "at risk" for failure of primary grade students, so that they could receive remedial measures. The intelligence test were developed for such measures which became wide spread. Intelligence means the ability frame of mind to solve problems that could he measured and its testing was called Intelligence Quotient or "IQ."

Gardner, a Harvard Psychologist provided the means of mapping these abilities that human possessed, by grouping them into eight categories or "intelligences" as follows. Each person possesses all eight intelligences. Some possess high levels and some have low levels.

1. **Linguistic Intelligence** – It is the ability to use the words effectively such as oration, story telling or writing found in editors, generalists and play writers.

   This intelligence could be enhanced by using lectures, group discussions, books, writing speeches, story telling, oral reading, memorizing, publishing etc. It is 'delt by brains' left temporal area, (broca's area)

2. **Logical – Mathematical Intelligence** – It is capacity to use numbers effectively found in mathematicians, accountants, statisticians, scientists & computer personal. Such intelligence can be developed by solving mathematical problems, questioning, creating codes, puzzles and games, calculations and scientific thinking. Left frontal and right parietal lobe of brain deal with such intelligence.

3. **Spatial Intelligence** – This intelligence deals with sensitivity to colour, shapes, space form and capacity to visualize visual or spatial ideas. Such intelligence could be improved by charts, graphs, diagrams, maps, photographs, slides, paintings, visual puzzles, ideas sketching graphics, computer graphics. Posterior part of right hemisphere of brain deals with this type of intelligence.

4. **Body Kinesthetic Intelligence** – This is the ability to use bodily expressions, and feelings which are found in actors, athletes, dancers & involve balancing coordination, flexibility, strength & speed. The skill can be acquired by the creative movements, competitive games, exercises, hand activities, tactile experiences, cooking, gardening & manipulative activities. These activities are controlled by motor cortex of brain and cerebellum and also basal ganglia.

5. **Musical Intelligence** – This is capacity to perceive musical forms such as sensitivity to rhythms, pitch, tone and understanding of music. The sense could be achieved by singing, humming, playing music in form of listening or in instrumental playing. Right temporal lobes are particularly sensitive to such intelligence

6. **Interpersonal Intelligence** – This is the ability to perceive and make distinction of mood, intensions, motivations, expressions of gestures and voices. For such developments one requires interpersonal

interactions, conflict resolutions, peer sharing, academic achievements, parties, social gathering and discrimination among different kinds of interpersonal clues. Frontal lobes and Temporal lobes and Lymbic systems is responsible for such activities.

7. **Intrapersonal Intelligence** – This type of intelligence deals with recognition of one's strengths and limitations, awareness of intensions, moods, capacity of self discipline and self esteems. It is encouraged by goal setting, personal connections, self studies and teaching. Frontal and parietal lobes of brain control such intelligence.

8. **Naturalist Intelligence** – It is the expertise in environment, flora and fauna and natural phenomena such as cloud formation, mountains, environment and discrimination between non living things such as cars, sneakers etc. This is improved by nature walks, aquariums, gardening, nature study, window learning. Left parietal lobe of brain is important for such discrimination.

4. 12. Early mental stimulation has better effect

It has been proved beyond doubt with many researches in animals that when stimulation was given in early life, they developed at more rapid rate of growth and became more intelligent compared to non stimulated ones. It was also seen that a rat from dull strain when given stimulus in early days behaved in a similar way as bright strain. They open their eyes earlier and gained the weight faster. This was the effect of enriched environment. The brain of rats of dull variety who were similar earlier when studied, showed heavier brain cortex and more brain cells as compared to nonstimulated siblings. The brain chemicals were also found increased.

Though it is not possible to do the same type of study in human infants but the results can be compared to human to large extent. **Early brain stimulation makes the differences by increasing size and chemical functioning of brain.**

How to create such intelligence

1. Focus on specific topics – Create programs for teachings

2. Ask questions to create thoughts

3. Consider possibilities

4. List everything that comes in mind

5. Select appropriate activities and set up action plans

6. Implement the plan

7. Most people can develop each intelligence to an adequate level of competency even all eight to a reasonably high level

8. Intelligences usually work together in complex ways, no intelligence exists by itself alone. For example to cook a meal one has to read recipe (linguistic), dividing the ingredients (mathematical), cooking to satisfying all family members (interpersonal) and satisfying own appetite (intrapersonal) Simultaneously for playing a game, one requires a body kinesthetic intelligence (to run, kick and catch) spatial intelligence (orientation of playground) arguing about dispute of games (linguistic and interpersonal) counting goals (mathematical skills)

4. 13. Intellectual capacity develops more so before eight years by age

By about late adolescent age, the IQ seems to stabilize, after which there is little change. The child develops his half of intellectual capacity by age of four years and most of it by eight years of age. So by eight years he develops 80% of his total intelligence capacity. After this age there is only 20% change regardless of stimulation given. The child after late adolescence continue to learn but he uses his capability in different way and his basic intelligence becomes static around this age. After this he may use his intellectual capacity to accumulate knowledge or productive work or he may not use it. That shows that first 4 years are most important and are equal to next thirteen years when his intellectual capacity will develop. During first four years the brain is growing at faster rate. This should be realized by parents and at this time learning in right direction is most important. Home environment at this age influences the child most for his educational and overall development.

London Board of Education in their study had found that IQ of children in the same family decreased from the youngest to the oldest. The youngest group was age of 4 to 6 years, had an average IQ of 90 points and the oldest children of 12 to 22 years of age had an average of 60 points only. This suggests that characters other than heredity are also at work.

4. 14. Time limit for easy activation of brain cells

Every living thing has its own life. Similarly the human brain is living and growing organ of human body which has its own survival time and has limits of physical capacities. One can assume that there may be a biological clock which determines this time period for its maximal activity, slowing and ultimately stop functioning. This can be explained by example that if a small child get head injury and his brain area responsible for speech or working of one limb get injured, his speech is lost and limb is not able to move. After trying for sometimes, new areas of speech and limbs movement develops and functioning may return after few months but in cases of adults, in whom these areas once destroyed find extremely difficulty for the return of functions as new areas are difficult to form because his brain may no longer possesses the capacity of rejuvenation. Learning can easily be acquired in early life. The things wrongly learnt are thus difficult to change. Such Children who start acquiring training of a particular hobby reach later on at the top as compared to the children who start learning late.

4. 15. The child is an explorer

A small child has a basic drive and curiosity to explore everything, that's how he learns. The people call this a bad habit of touching the things and he is often punished for getting into everything. In their exploratory habits few things may be disturbed from their places and few things are broken. Parents do not have much time to mend or replace them or to have new things. Hence the child is always denied to touch the things. Since toddler and pre-school children have urgent need of brain stimulation which they get by exploring the things such as trying to unlock the lock with keys or open the tap to see running water or open the drawer to see different things or reach dressing table to see what parents are using but cannot sit idle. Bright children in school are often understood as troublemakers in the class, because they require learning stimulation much. Avery small child becomes alert when he is shown a coloured object and tries to jump to catch it. Next time he also behaves in the same way to show his interest and gradually this interest wears off to other objects. Small children concentrate on one thing for short time and change to next to get more stimulation by concentrating at many different things. The child learns by seeing, touching, tasting, exploring, by breaking, by imitating, hearing, jumping, running, climbing and so on to masters that activity and proceeds to next things to conquer. There are sensory and motor stimuli by which he will not only learn but will be much happier and contented. The child who is left in a cot or play-pen crying is lot unsatisfied for his basic needs of stimulation. The child wants new excitement and novelty every time to learn, to satisfy his senses and curiosity and this drive is identified by psychologists as primary requirement of the child. Hence parents are advised to give their time to child for his basic needs.

4. 16. The child has inbuilt drive for competency

Researches have been undertaken by a scientist Jean Piaget in younger children aged three months. The child was laid in a cot, over which a rattle was hung by a string. The string was tied with child's hand. As by chance movement, the string was pulled and rattle produced the move. The child was delighted and tried to make the noise to listen the sound again.

A six months old baby whose head was covered by a piece of cloth, tried to remove it by hands and when he succeeded, he had overwhelming joy and laughter and wanted this to be done again and again. When he could not remove the cloths by hands, he jerked his head to remove it and when he succeeded in it, he had boundless joy and so had the parents. Thus the child tried to become competent in removing the cloths from his head.

You might have observed that while sitting on a cot or playpen, the child throws a toy on the floor and howls at you to fetch that for him. He again drops it and expect you to help him getting it. He does it again and again till you are cooperating with him. You will consider this action of the child as purposeless and will get annoyed but for the child, this drill is learning of grasping and releasing about falling object and impact noise.

The parents are advised to be patient and understanding and should help the child for acquiring such competency. This will be perception of observation for the child who is learning by repeated experiments and storing in brain which will help in development behavior later on.

A two to three years old child tries to open an attache case by a chick is amusing for him and he wants to do it again and again to master it. He spends about half an hour in running or climbing up and down the staircase, only the first two or three steps before being picked up by the parents to prevent the fall. He will try to zip and unzip the jacket many time to master it before putting in the cupboard. A five years old will play a jumping game and jump again and gain to master the activity. So the child is always determined to do by himself and gain the competency, no matter how difficult the task is, even to the point of exhaustion.

The child has inner need to get experience of perceptional and motor activities to develop his cortical area of the brain which after birth was very much ill equipped. This all is his drive for competency. All his later thought and activity will depend upon his learning at younger age. Thus he is programming his brain computer with all those perception and motor activities.

Many researches have proved that child has inbuilt drive for gaining competency. Dr. Montessori in her studies based her technique of education on this psychological basis for preschool children. She programmed in simple and logical ways to teach the children and as they became competent in one task, next job was taken up for learning. This feel of competency gives lot of joy to children to learn more and more.

4. 17. Create joy in learning and no pressure

As already described that child has inbuilt drive for learning and competency due to his curiosity and exploration. Thus learning should become a pleasure in younger age. The child works tirelessly without getting tired. Dr. Montessori based her creation in this way only. The child about four years of age is taught for one particular task and once the child masters it, next job is undertaken for teaching. Such activities are enjoyed by children and they learn them fast. In such learning and teaching external pressure is avoided.

But as the age advances and the child reaches in secondary education, his interest in learning gets distorted as now he is aware of the anxiety of examination and competitions, home-works and his tensions build up everyday. **He at this time becomes responsible for learning though he may not feel the joy and feels that he has to do some hard work to achieve his goal and he becomes committed to it. This is his motivation.** To achieve this commitment, his initial learning at younger stage should be pleasurable, joyful, without pressure and mental stimulating. The purpose of such learning activities is not to push the child into anxiety and pressure or to compete with a neighbouring child or to perform like a puppet but to make himself happy. Hence learning should be enjoyable informative to the interest of the child, to improve voluntary learning and not pressuring to push him with fear or punishment.

4. 18. Greater the variety of environmental stimuli, greater is the capacity for coping power

Dr. Piaget had observed that the child's intelligence increases if greater variety of environmental stimuli are given to him. Such stimuli trigger the basic functioning and development of brain. The child finds himself more capable of reacting intelligently to the environment and his potentials develop fast.

If there is lack of environmental stimuli, he is likely to suffer mentally and would decrease his intelligence and would not be fit to cope up with challenges in his environment.

The parent should match the education of the child to his environment and challenges and his growing abilities. One should not underestimate the child capacity of learning. The more new things the child observes, the more experience he gets and gets stimuli for coping them up.

4. 19. Acquiring other language

Language development is very complex phenomenon. The child's brain is conditioned to speak in that language whichever he has learnt. The child has got the capacity of learning second or even third language because the brain of the child has special functional characteristics. He can easily learn them in early lifetime while adults find it difficult to acquire the other languages, even though they are highly intelligent, well qualified and can never speak it without hesitation and correctness. That shows that brain of the child is better equipped for learning other languages as compared to adult. The child's brain records what he hears due to sensitivity of its nerve cells and also the child repeats it often. Around six years of age, the child can express in other language as well. For language development, the child has got the network in the brain which helps in recognizing, thinking, motor activity and speech. For other language, the child may use act of translation and this is called indirect learning. But if the child is taught the other language and explained in the same language, he establishes language units in his brain for that languages and it becomes easier for him to speak the same. Suppose the child is taught three languages at three different place such as home, school and nursery, he will try to deal with the persons in that language only whenever he is learning at that place, though he does not know what language he is using. After the age of eight years, the conditioning of the brain for the language becomes difficult but if he has already acquired some words of other language in his brain, he has to use translation process to learn the other language which is little difficult. Once the brain units for other language are made it becomes easier to speak the language later on even after long period of time.

In Europe, many languages are spoken at different places, the child may be listening the words of different language and it may become easier for him to pick up the other language.

4. 20. Existence of sensitive period for specific learning

Researchers believe that a certain mechanism is activated in child's brain at certain period of life which helps the child for specific learning. Right triggering at right time is important for such learning. This mechanism can not be stimulated at later dates and can only be activated at very early life time. This period in human babies is around six months when semisolid food can be introduced in such babies. Then the age of four to five years is also a sensitive period suggested by Dr. Montessori of Italy. She described the method of teaching in preschool children which shall be described in later chapters. She discovered that children at four to five years like reading, writing and understand mathematical concepts with great enthusiasm and ease. At this age the child also learns to speak some what fluently.

A child between the age of three and a half to four and a half years learns meaning of reading and writing more easily than at age of six to seven years. And if the child lacks in such study due to environment, living in remote village or slum area where there is less facilities of learning before age of six years of age, will remain handicapped in learning.

Children between the age of four to five years learn reading and writing easily and with great enthusiasm.

Speech —

Speech is complex process where seeing, hearing, thinking lip work, throat, breathing and tongue is involved, which require coordination while writing requires thinking and finger actions and is comparatively easier than speech. According to Dr. Montessori it is easier for children to control hand and finger and thus writing than speech.

Children at the age of three to four years imitate television images, songs, tunes. They can dance at those tunes, they can recognize passage around home, recognize the names of common animals and objects and memorize the books which they had gone three to four times through it and even they are able to do some work on computer and art colouring and painting.

The child who is eager to learn, reading and writing around age of four years, may be this is sensitive period for him for such activity.

The sensitive periods in a child helps in development of sense of order in which he insists for routine that the child should have the same seat while eating on table chair. He should have same glass, plate and spoon as he is already using. He or she would like to have doll or toy before going to sleep and would like to sleep at the same chosen place. The child may be in the habit of having a bottle for feed and TV on for his sleep and so on. Most parents consider this period as a nuisance but at this age brain of the child is trying to form generalization from the made observations and they insist on routine. **The parents at this time should inculcate good working and learning habits, games in which the child finds greater satisfaction. They are also advised to be watchful when the child is more eager and interested is learning.**

4. 21. The child's brain can be compared with a computer

In our previous chapter we have focused on the brain and its working (Chapter 2) we have mentioned that the brain has outer grey thick layer known as cortex which comprises of millions of nerve cells and that certain parts of the brain have fixed areas for a particular function. The sensory organs such as eyes, ears, nose, tongue, skin collect sensory information from the environment and change into electrical signals which are transmitted to the nerve cells of cortex through nerve fibres. The nerve cells thus get activated and the information is stored there in. This memory is used for action.

The areas in the cortex are chiefly used for memory. These may be speech, or other senses, motor activity such as writing, walking, swimming, running and so on or reading. If during the operation certain areas are touched with mild electrical stimuli, the patient if concious can remember the past memory. This is how all programming of the brain takes place like a computer.

The information thus stored in cortex is used by brain and is utilized in thoughts which are governed by intelligence. This memory is converted into action when desired, like that of computer which shows the programmes on the screen.

This is not fully understood as to how at desired time one remembers the things and how brain takes the information out.

Hence whatever is recorded in the brain like computer can be retrieved as later stage.

05   # Joy of Parenthood

Joy of Parenthood

"I love him not because he is good, but because he is my little child"

– Rabindra Nath Tagore

5. 1. From parent's diary

Even before the baby was born, the thoughts of having it in the family, our own creation, how would he or she look like, me or my husband, the hopes, the expectations, were source of tremendous joy to both of us. When it was just born and handed over to me, I forgot all my labour pains seeing that heavenly, innocent and nascent creation lying beside me, the joy was of my whole being. The feeling of solemn determination to bring him up in the best possible way, may it be beyond our means, over powered my mind. We tried our best to keep up to this determination right from the day one. The feeling of satisfaction and joy while breast feeding my baby, cannot be described in words. The smile of the baby in response to our own words and gestures used to make us so happy that we ignored the sleepless nights and physical tiredness undergone. His each moment was our moment. Our life started revolving around him. Why? was it because of some expectations? not the least, it was the parental love, the selfless love expecting nothing in return to balance it, the love associated with the joy of parenthood. Each milestone of the baby gave so much joy that we used to talk about it to everyone in the family. Afterwards he started sitting, calling mama-papa, crawling, standing, walking and so on. The happiness derived from each of these activities is so deeply engraved in our hearts that we even can recollect these memories in our old age and derive extreme joy even today.

When he grew up, our total involvement in his studies, in his holistic growth and his well being was quite natural because somewhere beneath these worries and tensions, was the joy of parenthood.

A Family

His academic and other achievements became our achievements. Even when he grew up as an adult individual and separated from us, the recollection of the past memories of his childhood, his laughter, birthdays, school days give us joy till today. Our blessings to the child too are full of joy parenthood. He has been a gifted child as he was well liked by his school children and people around and was elected to school office. He had leadership qualities and ranked high in his school and college. How these years have passed, we just remember that it is only sometime back that we used to carry him in our arms and now we receive his letters from distant places, which we keep under our mattress and read them one by one, again and again. Is it not the joy of parenthood? In our minds, how he is eating? Is he happy? These concerns and worries also depict the joy. However, sometimes we do think of those persons who have never experienced the joy of parenthood, then we feel grateful to the almighty for being blessed with all the wealth of life "the joy of parenthood." Now is the time for our children to experience the same. This is how the wheel of life keeps on moving.

5. 2. An advice for parents

As we know the girls are initially faster than boys. Girls catch their milestone earlier as compare to boys. The babies who are advanced in their physical activities may be very slow in teething and vice versa. The children who turn out later to be smart in school work may have slow beginning to talk, that their parents become afraid for a while that they were slow children of ordinary intelligence are sometime very early talkative. Initially there may be mixed rates of development and each child is composed of individual pattern of growth. **Loving and enjoying the child for what they look like, for what they do and**

forgetting about qualities what they do not have, is an important practical point and should be the joy of parenthood. The parents job is to love, enjoy and fill them with confidence, they will have spirit that will be make the best of all capabilities they have. They will be benefited by all opportunities that come on their way and will become brighter everyday.

If the child gets good mental stimulation and encouraging home environment, he is likely to progress towards achievements. It will be classed as intelligent with superior IQ. Parent can raise almost every child of moderate intelligence to a superior intelligence by substantial degree of warm home environment and proper mental stimulation at an early age, regardless of his inherited genes. Such children consistently do better, learn more and faster than their counter-parts. Researchers are of the opinion that those school children who were rated as bright and mentally superior had stimulating and warm home atmosphere planned by parents at younger age of birth onwards.

Researchers at university of Chicago by Dr. Robert indicate that boys and girls who are mentally superior come from where the school and home atmosphere is congenial, stimulating and family member enjoy learning, set examples, in attaining higher education and where the child is trained at an early age for the desired direction of achievement.

On the country, if the child is of biological superior family but does not get adequate early stimulation in school or home will not develop as a bright child.

Everyone wants bright children in their family with superior IQ and such a child to have multiple qualities. Such children are better adjusted in family and are emotionally stable as compared to average children. They have less emotional problem and have better capacity to cope up with the problems.

Gifted children are usually popular amongst their classmates and people around like them. They possess leadership quality and also good in extra curricular activity. They have high ability to make friends with peer group whose IQ is 40–50 points lower. They participate in sports and social activity more than average child, have good sense of humor, appreciate more jokes and are lot more happier and enthusiastic. We do not mean to say that children of average intelligence do not have such qualities. They also have lots of good qualities as mentioned above which can further be developed. Brighter child have less of diseases and are average in coordination, weight, height and personality. They score high in originality and creativity and can do better in music and art.

They are often self sufficient and cause fewer problems for parents, have less undesirable personality traits and are dependable, having initiatives and find their own way to fulfill the tasks. Such children adjust better in stress situation and are conscientious, trust-worthy and follow the rules of discipline. They always have the focus towards their goals by solving the problems.

Many of such very gifted children who have very high IQ feel superior, proud and may not be able to adjust on the jobs very well. Though they are genious but do not get along easily and happily with other persons and feel very much disturbed about injustice. This is because of very thin line between very high intelligence and madness exists. If not controlled properly, they become mischievous and trouble makers.

Parents should always understand the need of gifted children, may it be social or emotional to give them the right way. On the whole bright and gifted children are happier and productive, having fewer problems, well adjusted, well liked, joyful and achievers.

Parent would always feel to have such gifted children and it would be worth putting efforts to give them mentally stimulating first six to eight years and giving them right discretion which will give them maximum joy in their lives.

These are few gridlines for parents to raise their children smart and intelligent.

1. **Controlling environment** – The parents must understand the child's behaviour towards effective parenting. The parents usually teach the child to behave which may be sometimes unrealistic and leads to ineffective method of encouraging them. The child may reactun-appropriately for following reasons:

    a. They do not know how to behave in certain situations because they might have not been taught.

    b. The child may be sick, tired or hungry or may be defending himself.

    c. They are developmentally not mature enough to learn type of expected behaviour.

Controlling the physical environment, not the child makes task much easier. For example if a one year old child becomes mobile and tries to investigate even dangerous things such as electrical points, it is better to cover those points rather than teach him to keep away. Similarly such a child puts everything into the mouth, it is easier to keep small objects out of his reach.

2. **Believe in positive commands** – Give positive information to the child and not a negative one, such as you can put your dirty clothes in the washing machine rather than do not put the clothes here and there.

3. **Be firm, kind and consistent** – The child feels more secure if he feels that parents are always in charge. Set the limits. He should know that you mean, what you say.

4. **Appreciate your child** – Take notice of positive behaviour of the child and not only negative. Children quickly learn that negative behaviour gets attention and it better to have some attention rather than no attention. Hence acknowledge positive behaviour and encourage the child on such behaviours. Do not use "do not" statement, use positive ones.

5. **Honour your child's impulse** – Very young children do not understand values, they are egocentric which leads to problem. Set the limits.

6. **Establish family values** – Such as gentleness, respectful to each other, say prayers together etc.

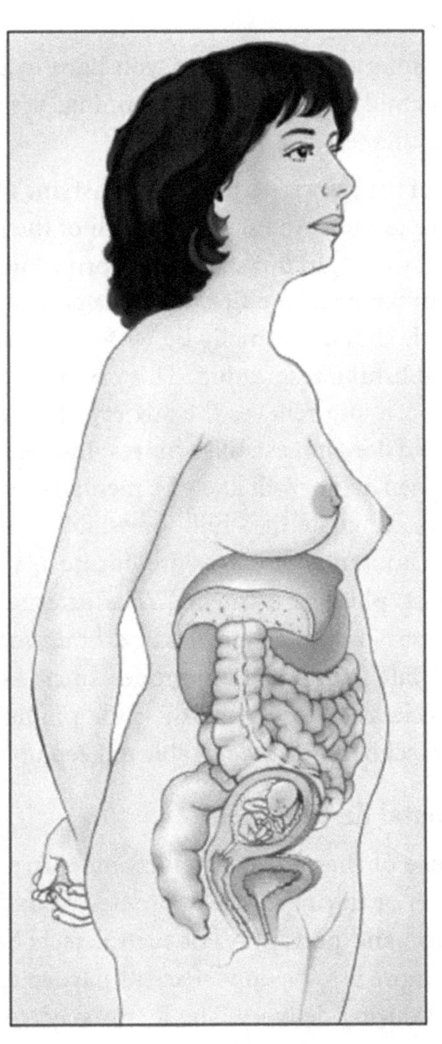

To make your child smart and intelligent, you have to take care of pregnant mother and unborn child from the very beginning. We should be discussing the care in following chapters.

The first glimps of the baby is exciting and satisfying for all family members and everyone is eager to know the sex and health of the baby and the mother. The baby may be a boy or a girl but should be normal and healthy, is the most important concern of parents. The first vigorous cryis most important in the life of newborn which should normally be within first sixty seconds of birth and is helpful in establishing respiration. This cry from delivery room signals the arrival of a newborn and relieves the anxiety of mother, family members and relative. If the child does not establish his respiration in first 60 seconds, his brain will not get oxygen and he will likely be mentally retarded. Doctors in the delivery room always stimulate the child for establishment of his respiration during this period. Thousands of babies are born every years. Some of them may have some defect, physical or mental. The external physical defects are easy to detect but internal physical defects and brain malfunctioning are not identified until much later, until their milestones, such as smiling, headholding, sitting, walking, speech, are delayed and the child might be unable to take his own care later and in school they are not able to keep up with his classmates.

6. 1. Threats to foetal development

There are many cause of these defects which may occur before child's birth in the mother's womb or during delivery or after birth. Lot of researches are going on for detection and prevention of such defects before birth as well as during birth and lot more is to be done. Parents have to exercise much care for an unborn child and during delivery. The foetus stays for nine months in the womb and our aim should be that the birth of that baby should be uneventful and he should take birth with good brain, hence both the aspects of care of baby before birth and during the delivery are very important. Organ system of unborn is most affected during periods of maximum growth and organ differentiation, generally during first three months when the organs of the child are developing, particularly if mother is exposed to various toxic agents.

The unborn child receives its nutrition from the mother hence care of the mother is of utmost importance. Inherited disorders, chromosomal disorder and congenital malformation, conceptions disorder, drugs (mercury thalidomide, antiepileptics) chemicals, hypothyroidism, genetic mutations, sexually transmitted diseases, contagious and infectious diseases, injuries, smoking, alcoholism, malnutrition and high temperature all have bad effects on the brain of the child and can also lead to abortion or premature birth. Still there are certain unknown causes of birth defects beyond medical prevention. Based on current knowledge, we can improve the chances of good quality and healthy brains in the child by some general rules which shall be described in the subsequent text.

Threat to unborn is highest during early pregnancy period. About 30% of the pregnancies end in spontaneous abortions, most often during first trimester. In some countries foetal alcohol syndrome is quite high.

Most of the women wait until they are quite sure of their two missed period, for having a pregnancy. Baby's major organs have been formed during that period and much of the most crucial time of development has already passed. If a mother has regular menses and there is a missed period she should get herself checked for pregnancy which is quite easy these days. Checking blood for pregnancy (HCG) is the most sensitive and specific pregnancy test at two weeks after conception. Urine test for detection of pregnancy is also available. The tests are done by simple kits and take only few minute. Ultrasound examination can also detect the embryo at 6–8 weeks that is 2 weeks after expected period.

There are many mechanism involved in development of foetus and birth of a child. Many of these mechanisms are unknown. An increasing number of disorders can be detected through prenatal diagnosis by blood examination, ultrasound, amniocentesis and villous biopsy.

Such information may help the family to make decision about the pregnancy. All possible intervention options may be put forth including termination of pregnancy.

Successful prevention requires prompt prenatal diagnosis and sophisticated management end specific therapies. The central theme of all the efforts is to prevent mental retardation, promotion of healthy brain development and providing growth promoting environment.

We feel that the mother must be conversant with the knowledge of foetal development in uterus, planning of the baby and other aspects of healthy

development of brain of foetus. We shall discuss some common aspects about the same in the following text.

6. 2. Foetal growth in uterus during pregnancy

The intrauterine life starts with a single cell that is formed from the fusion of egg (ovum) and the sperm. By the fifth week, the time when the women first realizes, she might be pregnant, the fertilized egg has settled in the womb lining and the embryo has already begun to develop into various tissues and organs of the baby, such as the heart, brain and the muscles. The brain starts developing during 1st week and gross structure of brain is established by 8 weeks but its nerve connection continue to develop throughout pregnancy thus makes it vulnerable to drugs, lack of oxygen and other threats throughout.

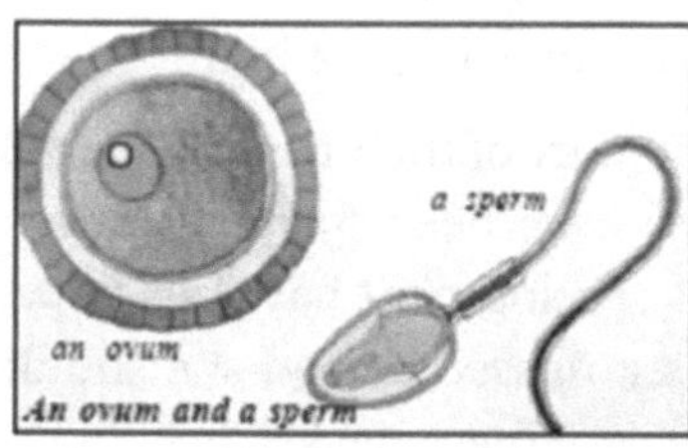

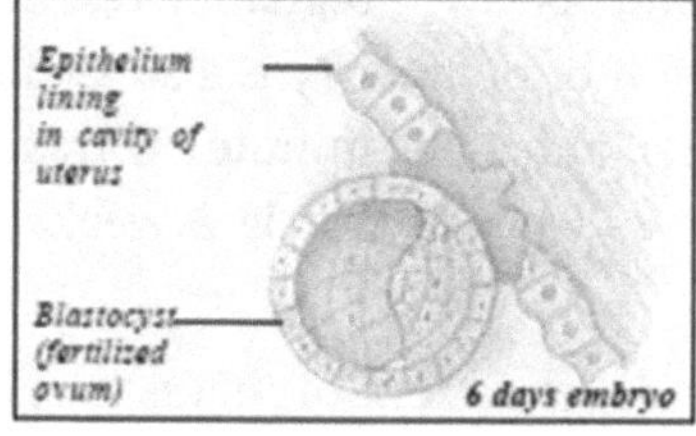

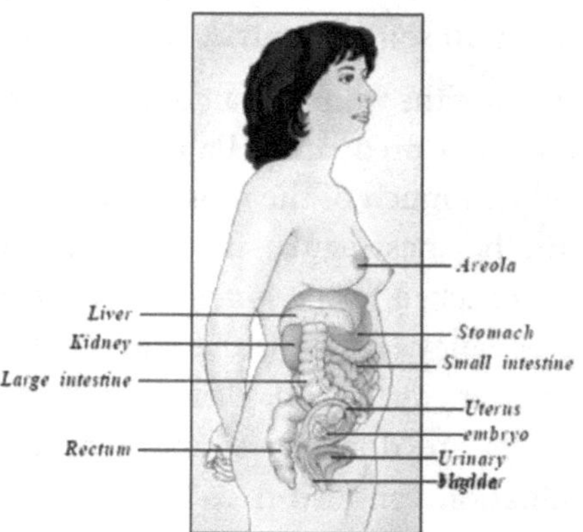

Eight Weeks Embryo in Uterus
(1st Trimester)

Gestational Age (Weeks)	Approx. Weight of Foetus (gms)
10	5–8
20	300–460
30	1500
40	2500–3000

Foetal weight gain in uterus – The embryo is about 2.5 cm by the end of eight weeks. Eyes, mouth, ears, umbilical cord, hands and feet, ovaries and testes can be identified. The foetal period starts at 9 weeks of pregnancy when organ systems start remodelling. The length at this time is 5 cm and weight is 8 gms. However, foetus becomes viable after 20 weeks when weight being 460 gm and length 19 cm. By the end of 12 weeks, all organ systems are fully formed but foetal movements are still weak. The first 3 months of pregnancy (First trimester) being crucial for organ formation and are vulnerable to X-rays and medicines, which may damage the organ development. Between 16–20 weeks (early 2nd trimester) the mother can feel her baby's movement for the first time as a slight fluttering or floating movement. It is important to note down this date as it helps to recheck the expected date of delivery.

During second trimester the baby grows fast. Nails, eye brows and eye lashes appear. The eyes, however, remain close until about 26 weeks. The body of the baby becomes covered with fine hair which shed before or soon after birth.

During the last 3 months of pregnancy, the baby grows and builds up energy reserves. The weight increases to 2500 gm or more and, length upto 50 cm. The movements are more vigorous even in response to touchingto the mother's abdomen or noise. By about 34 weeks, the baby's head moves down into pelvis of the mother, this is said to be as "engaged." Sometimes it may not engage until labour has started.

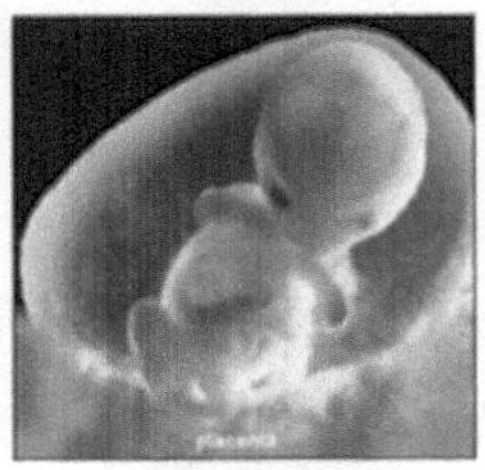

8 Weeks Embryo
(ultrasound)

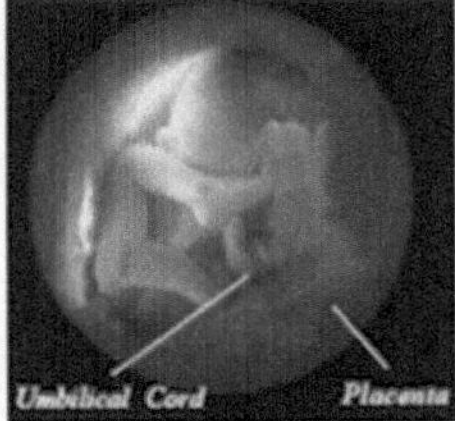

28 Weeks Foetus
(ultrasound)

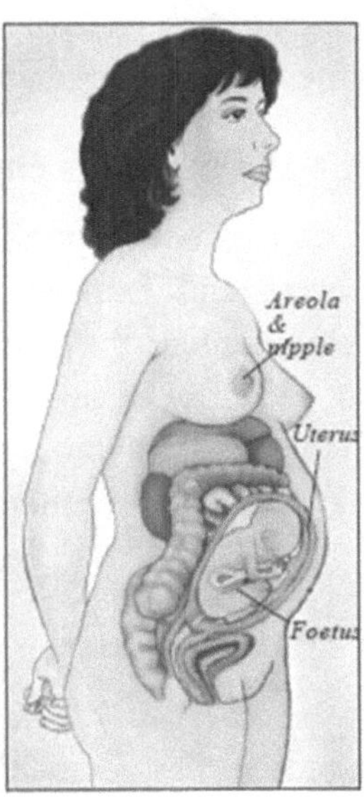

2nd Trimester
(13–28 wks)

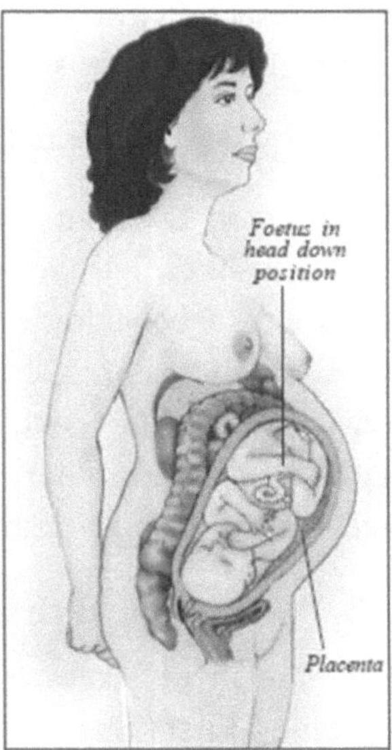

3rd Trimester
(29–40 wks)

6. 3. The placenta

The foetus lies in a sac of watery liquid known as amniotic fluid which cushions it within the womb. It's life support system is the placenta, a mass of tissue containing foetal blood vessels, which lies bathed in the maternal circulation. The foetus is attached to placenta by unbilical cord.

How does oxygen and nutrition pass to foetus from mother?

Oxygen and nutrients pass into the foetal blood vessels and carbon dioxide and other waste products from the foetus are returned to the mother. Placenta is not a barrier in real sense as most of the drugs, hormones and toxic substances such as infections can pass through to foetus from the mother. The blood passes from foetus to placenta and back through blood vessels in the umbilical cord, which is attached to baby's abdomen. Foetal and mother's blood do not get mixed in placenta because there is thin membrane which separates the blood of mother and the foetus and this membrane allows food, medicines and excretions to pass through it.

6. 4. Behaviour development

The foetal behavior is clearly affected by maternal medication, diet and oxygen. Foetal movements also increase in response to a sudden sound and decrease after several repetition. This ability to habituate to repeated stimuli is a form of learning and is diminished in mentally impaired and stressed fetuses.

6. 5. Effects of environment and mother's emotions on her baby

The parents transmit their excessive competitiveness to their children. Anxieties, likes, dislikes, phobias and fears–all have stress reaction and contribute in behavioral development of the baby and he is likely to have similar temperament. There is conditioned learning in the womb. Similarly drugs, alcohol and watching violence have stress effects on the baby. Music, contentment and mother's other joyful environmental influences have positive effects on the growing baby.

6. 6. Psychological changes in the mother

There are three stages in the mother's psychological development during pregnancy. First stage is when mother first learns that she is pregnant. Elation at the thought of producing a baby, wish of perfect parent, fears of inadequacy and other problems of parental relationship intensify. The second stage begins when mother becomes aware of infants movements (quickening) at around 20 weeks. This palpable evidence of existence of foetus heightens the mother's feelings. During third stage at the end of third trimester towards the end of pregnancy, the mother becomes aware of patterns of foetal activity and begins to ascribe to her foetus an individual personality and ability to survive independently. Old conflicts may surface as woman psychologically identifies with her own mother. Parents worry about foetus's healthy development. They may be reassured by ultrasonic and ammiotic fluidexamination.

6. 7. Plan your child when you are between the age of 21 years and 35 years

(a) Pre-marriage planning

The planning for the healthy parenthood starts before the marriage. It is now well known that marriage between the close relatives can lead to certain inheritable diseases in the offspring such as haemophilia, thalassemia (blood disease), spinal defects, brain and neuromuscular diseases. It is because either or both male and female partners may be the carriers of a particular disease which gets expressed in their baby, therefore such marriages are not advisable and should be discouraged. It is better to know about the familial diseases before marriage, considering not only the parents of the couple but also the grandparents and close relatives like uncles and aunts. There are certain tests that would be helpful in finding out some traits in tie both partners before marriage.

Various tests advised before marriage

    a.   Tests for chromosomal disorders and genetic screening

    b.   Tests for bone defects

    c.   Test for blood defects like thalassemia and haemophilia

    d.   Test for muscular dystrophies

    e.   Exposure to drugs of abuse, chemicals and radiation causing genetic mutation (gene modification)

    f.   Tests for AIDS, sexually transmitted diseases & hepatitis B & C.

In India, these tests are available in some hospitals. Few years back people did not pay much attention about such things and became parents. Since these days the families are small and have limited income hence the urban families are going in a planned way for having limited number of children. The best time for planning marriage is between 21–26 of age. However for girls is 18 yrs and boys 21 yrs or above.

There are some families in which child marriages are solemnized when the children are small and immature and they even do not understand the meaning of marriage. Such marriages should not be recognized. The usual practice of arranged marriage is good practice but marriage in close relatives is not advisable. Very early marriages lead to misarranges, foetal malformation and premature births.

(b) Genetic counseling

With the help of screening, genetic counseling and few medical tests before marriage, certain genetic disorders can be prevented in a planned marriage and pregnancy. If such counseling is not made use of, then the chances of multiple diseases shall exist which are very difficult or impossible to treat. These include chromosomal and genetic diseases like Down's syndrome, diseases of bone and blood, diseases of spine, muscles, metabolic and bio-chemical deficiency diseases etc. If there is history of inherited diseases or birth defects in previous pregnancies or in family, mother's age is over 35 years or she has two or more abortions, it is important to seek medical advice for planning pregnancy. One of the biggest risk in elderly mother is birth of child suffering from Down's Syndrome (Mongolism) which is produced by chromosomal defect. The normal number of chromosome in human is 46 which are paired for 1–22 with two sex chromosomes. Down's syndrome children have extra chromosome (three copies of chromosome 21) suffer from mental retardation and other defects. The extra chromosome which may be due to mistake in production of ovum in elderly mother before conception. Similarlyelderly father can also be affected in production of sperms.

One in 2500 women between child bearing age of 21–35 years may have Mangol baby but chance in elderly women is one in 100. Young parents are now advised to have chromosomal studies.

(c) Planning after marriage

After marriage, the couple plans for pregnancy. Pregnancy is a natural phenomenon and should not be considered as illness. Nevertheless, it needs proper planning, knowledge about the body changes and significance of medical supervision and expert advice which will be given in the following chapters. It is good to stop pills three months before the pregnancy and let the menstrual periods become normal otherwise chances of malformations in the child are likely to increase. Chronic diseases like anaemia, diabetes mellitus, high blood pressure, epilepsy, hormone abnormalities, psychiatric illness and heart diseases should be adequately treated before conceiving. To avoid the risks of birth disorders, prenatal screening is advised.

(d) Prenatal screening and diagnosis

Prenatal screening in the mother is undertaken to avoid the risk of birth disorders in the child. Certain tests are advised in the following conditions if:-

1. Age of the girl at the time of marriage is more than 35 years.

2. The husband and the wife are first cousins.

3. One or both partners or close family members (Parents/brother/ sister/aunt/uncle) suffered from any of the following genetic disorders such as thalassemia, haemophilia, spinabifida, meningo-myelocoele, anencephaly/small head, cleft palate and hare-lip, Down's syndrome or other chromosomal disorders, cardiac anomalies and metabolic disorders.

(e) Repeated abortions/still births

Prenatal diagnostic test is done depending upon the specific, genetic disorder. The use of ultrasound gives information about anatomic abnormalities such as neural tube defects, hydrocephalus, limb abnormalities, congenital heart diseases and bone defects etc. Amnio-centesis in which liquor amnii is tested between sixteen to eighteen gestational weeks and chorionic villus in first terimestor are used for analysis of chromosomal abnormalities, bio-chemical disorders and DNA studies. Maternal blood or serum is also used for diagnosis of various diseases.

THE HEALTH OF PARENTS IS AN IMPORTANT FACTOR. A HEALTHY MOTHERIS LIKELY TO GIVE BIRTH TO A HEALTHY CHILD.

6. 8. Choose your doctor

Mrs. Vanita and her husband shifted from Bombay to Pune just two months back. She was pregnant and had a child of four years. None of either thought to take prenatal care before. Though she planed her delivery in the hospital but she might have some complication before delivery, she had never thought of.

Madame Jasmin is also pregnant and wishes to have second baby, her previous child is mentally retarded. During her first delivery she never bothered to see the specialists doctor and during delivery she had many problems at that time. Her child took lot of time for respiration, though he was resuscitated by child specialists.

If Jasmine had bothered to be in care of a specialists lady doctor and a child specialists, her first child would have not been mentally retarded. May it be first or third child, parents need care of specialists throughout the pregnancy and delivery period. It is important for the mother as well as baby.

While choosing the lady doctor and child specialists, the parents have to look for their qualifications, their confidence, professional ability, way of expression, bedside manners, temperament and experience and availability. All are very important aspects. Doctor has to be ethical and should be able to convey the truth about the problem. This aspect has special importance in parent – doctor relationship which builds up trust amongst them. "Good ethics start with good facts."

The doctor-patient relationship should be such that parent should not feel heritant in contacting the doctor anytime personally or by phone. Once you contact the doctor, giver her/him relevant details of your record and reference number. If doctor is not available in emergency, contact a hospital or nursing home. The parents need to trust their doctors for not declaring the private information to others. There is an implied promise by a doctor not to disclose without the consent of the parents. The qualified healers do not have scientific background and may cause more harm than good.

During visit to specialists doctor, the women should register herself with the doctor as follows.

6. 9. Registration and antenatal care

Mother should register herself under the care of a competent obstetrician for her antenatal (prior to delivery) care, which includes regular assessment of foetal growth and well- being, progress of pregnancy, timely detection and treatment of complications and maintaining good health during pregnancy.

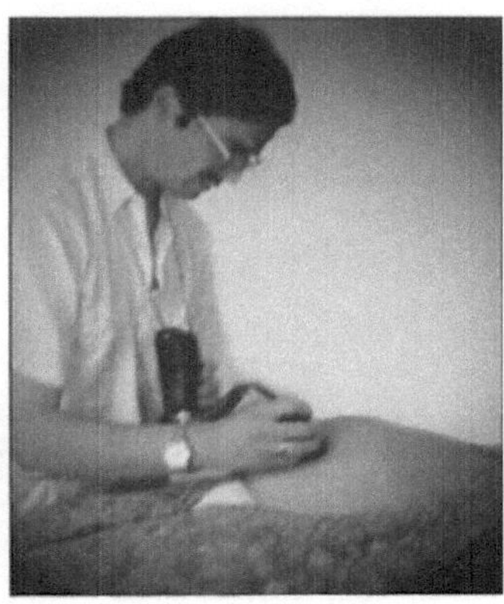

Ante-natal Examination

When to register?

Pregnant mother should register around three months after her last monthly menstrual period. However, if the woman has problems such as feeling unwell or any medical problem (diabetes mellitus, hypertension, chronic illness) or has had difficulties or complications during her past pregnancies, she should get registered earlier and also consult her physician.

6. 10. Antenatal care – why it is required?

At registration, the mother is given an antenatal card, which contains important information about her health and pregnancy. She should keep this record carefully and carry this whenever she goes for antenatal check up or for medical check up or other ailments during pregnancy. The purpose of antenatal care is to ensure normal pregnancy and labour and delivery of a healthy baby.

6. 11. Frequency of antenatal visits

Once a month from 12 to 28 weeks, once a fortnight till 36 weeks, and once a week till time of delivery. If the mother has a problem, she may be asked to attend more often. On subsequent antenatal visits, the mother will be asked about her general health and her weight, BP and urine will be checked. The abdomen will be examined to see the foetal growth, foetal position, movements and heart rate. Sometimes ultra - sound scan is done to check the growth of the baby or to determine the due date and anomalies. Mother is given health education at each antenatal visit.

Tetanus immunization

During pregnancy two injections of tetanus toxoid are given, six weeks apart, usually during 6th and 8th months. It protects the baby from tetanus neonatorum.

6. 12. Changes in body weight during pregnancy

The changes in body weight of the mother during pregnancy are as follows:

Duration of pregnancy (weeks)	Weight gain (kgs)
0–12	1.0
12–16	1.0
17–20	2.0
21–24	2.0
25–28	2.0
29–32	1.5
33–36	1.5
37–40	1.0
Total 40 weeks	**12.0 kgs**

The above gain in weight in the pregnant women is due to the foetus and placenta (5 kg), uterus enlargement (1 kg), breast enlargement (1 kg), fat and protein storage in the body (4 kg) and fluid retention (1–1.5 kg).

6. 13. Maternal factors and diseases affecting the unborn child

Many conditions in the mother which can harm the unborn child can be prevented, checked and treated by specialist doctor. Anaemia, Urine infection, vaginal infection, diabetes mellitus, Thyroid disease, foetal malformations, ectopic pregnancy, size of the child, position of placenta in uterus, hepatitis infection, AIDS, Syphilis infection can be detected and treated before development of complications.

There is great relationship of prenatal care to mental retardation and birth defects and mother may be at risk. Doctor assesses the risk factors in the pregnant woman and the unborn child. He or she may order for certain test to confirm the problem.

6. 14. Foetal well being assessment in pregnancy

Foetal life begins with completion of organ formation at about 12 weeks of pregnancy. Environment and genetic factors influence the development.

(A) Assessment of poetal growth – It is assessed by either gestational age, by dating of last menstrual period or by ultrasound examination at 12 weeks or more so between 18–20 weeks, in which serial determination of biparietal diameter is most important (head circumference), head to abdomen circumference ratio and total intrauterine volume measurement are taken. Serial examination are required for assessments.

(B) Assessment of foetal maturity – The assessment of maturity is made by:

    i.   Determination of amniotic fluid surfactant contents, creatinine and lecithin.

    ii.   Extent of calcification of bones by ultrasound.

    iii.   Detection of first audible foetal heart sound (16–18 weeks).

    iv.   Initial foetal movements (18–20 weeks).

Tests advised during pregnancy

There are some routine tests and some special tests advised during pregnancy by the doctor.

Blood: Tests are carried out for haemoglobin, peripheral smear, total WBC and differential counts, test for ABO, Rh grouping, thalassaemia, haemophilia, HIV, VDRL, blood sugar, hepatitis B carrier and AIDS. Blood urea and creatinine are also estimated and Coomb's test if the mother is Rh negative.

Urine: Test for sugar is done on first visit and also on subsequent visits, if sugar remains positive on more than one visit; she is referred to medical specialist for confirmation of diabetes mellitus, as it has to be very carefully controlled during pregnancy. Tests for urinary proteins and pus cells are done to exclude renal disease/ infection. "At risk" factors are clearly mentioned on the card, these relate to mother's age, weight, physical fitness, experience of previous pregnancy and delivery and need for special care.

Ultrasound: By ultrasound examination, mother can see her baby on screen. It is painless and safe procedure done by putting transducer over mother's abdomen /vagina. Normally pregnant woman undergoes three scans during pregnancy.

    1.   **6–8 weeks** – Dating scan (2 weeks after her menstrual expected period).

    2.   **16–20 weeks** – To detect foetal anomalies.

    3.   **35 to 36 weeks** – To know about foetal well-being.

Special Tests – These tests are advised only when birth defects are suspected

1. Rubella titre for TORCH infections
2. Chromosomal studies
3. MRI/CT scan
4. Amniocentesis (16–18 weeks) for genetic disorders
5. Chorionic villous biopsy-for genetic disorders
6. Foetal blood sampling
7. Endoscopy
8. Maternal serum alpha foeto-proteins (16 weeks)—for brain and spinal cord defects
9. Human chorionic gonadotropins
10. Other hormones estimations – Thyroid harmones, Pituitary harmone

6. 15. Healthy motherhood for healthy newborn

The unborn totally depends upon his/her mother for nutrition and protection for about nine months of existence. For which mother has to maintain her nutrition and health. That means the diet of mother should be balanced containing all building blocks of the body. Woman who have inadequate diet, have more miscarriages, more still born babies and more premature babies as compared to well nourished.

It is important to keep good health during pregnancy because the mother is responsible for her baby's health, for which good nutrition and good life style and exercises is required.

(a) Nutrition

A healthy diet is one of the most important factor affecting the health of mother and child. Many health problems are due to poor diet during pregnancy. The diet should be well balanced containing proteins, carbohydrates, fats, minerals, (calcium, iron) and vitamins (Vit-A, B complex, C and D). The caloric requirement during pregnancy is around 2500 Kcal and during lactation, it is about 3000 Kcal.

Healthy Diet

Daily diet must contain one litre of milk, 1–2 slices of cheese, one egg, 120–200 gm of meat or fish, liver/kidney, green and fresh salad, fruits, green vegetables, bread, cereals, pulses, butter or oil. The fluid intake (water, juice, tea etc.) should be 6–8 glasses per day. Iodized table salt 5–10 gms/day is essential. Iron, Vit-D and calcium are prescribed after 12 weeks of pregnancy to prevent anaemia and osteomalacia. Fish like salmon, sardine and trout may be taken twice a week. Folic acid 400 microgram me should be taken each day starting from a week before pregnancy, till twelve week of pregnancy, it helps in preventing neural tube defects. It is present in leafy vegetables & black eyed beans.

Diet and calories/day requirement during pregnancy

Agent	Amount required/ day	Agent	Amount required/ day
Milk	Two-Three Glasses	Green vegetable.	150 gms
Cheese	Thirty gms	Fruits	150 gms
Curd	Three-four Table Spoonful/meal	*Egg	One
Lentil (Dal)	Three-Four Table Spoonful/meal	Nuts (almonds)	25–30 in number
Chapati	Six or equivalent rice	*Chicken/Fish/ Meat	100–150 gms
Total Calories/day 2500 Kcal.		(* for non-vegetarians)	

Nutrients – their sources and effects on mother and foetus

Nutrients	Sources	Effects
Proteins	Milk and its products, Pulses, Egg, Meat and Fish	For energy, tissue building & repair, growth and immunity
Fats	Milk, butter, butter oil, nuts	Energy producing, hormones-formation, absorption of fat soluble vitamins
Carbohydrates	Rice, Wheat, Potatoes,	Energy producing
Calcium	Milk and its products, green leafy vegetables, fish, egg.	Growth of bones & teeth, proper function of nervous system
Iron	Green leafy vegetables, dates, Apple, Guava	Prevents anaemia
Vitamin A	Milk and its products, Carrot, Fish, Meat	Eyes vision, integrity of skin and mucous lining.
Vitamin D	Vit-D-fortified milk & products, liver oil, fish, exposure to sunlight.	Growth of bones and teeth
Vitamin C	Citrus fruits, Tomato, Green vegetables	Maintains intercellular material, prevents scurvy, helps iron absorption.
Vitamin E	Fruits, egg, sunflower-seed, green vegetables	Helps blood circulation, anti-oxidant
Vitamin B-Complex	Milk, Cereals, legumes, nuts, eggs, fish, meat, vegetables	Various metabolisms, prevent anaemia, beri-beri, pellagra, skin disorders, fits

Mother should eat balance diet, she should eat high fibre diet which includes guar, barley, oats legumes, beans, peas and lentils, fruits and green vegetables to avoid constipations. **Frequent eating and avoiding starvation is important.**

Should a pregnant woman take diet for two – Pregnant women neither needs a special diet nor she is required to eat for two. The woman should take 300–500 calories extra than usual in her final weeks.

(b) What should be avoided by expectant mother?

i. **Smoking** – results in premature, low weight babies, increased chances of abortions and malformed babies

ii. **Alcohol** – Alcohol consumption causes low birth weight problems in baby.

iii. **Drugs** – Drugs except prescribed by the doctor.

iv. **Infections** – Typhoid, malaria, influenza, toxoplasmosis, rubella, cytomegalovirus infection, chicken pox and sexually transmitted diseases.

v. **Allergic foods** – All food items which cause asthma, eczema during pre-pregnancy period.

vi. **Coffee**

vii. **Other foods** – (a) Soft ripened cheese (goat's or sheep's milk cheese) leads to listeriosis. (b) Ready to eat poultry products unless thoroughly reheated.

viii. **Exposure to X-rays.**

For prevention of Toxoplasmosis – Wash your hands after handling cats and kittens, raw meat, and after gardening to avoid toxoplasmosis. Wash vegetable and salad to remove soil or cat faces.

(c) Special diets

What are iron rich foods – If mother is vegetarian and is anaemic, she should take iron rich food such as spinach, black-eyed beans, apple, guava, amla, dates, whole meal bread and pulses. Iron is readily absorbed in presence of vitamin C rich food such as citrus fruits and tomatoes. Tea and coffee inhibit iron absorption.

Non-vegetarian diet such as meat, poultry and fish contain fair amount of iron. Cooking in iron pans adds some iron to the food but destroys vitamin C.

Diet during morning sickness – The morning sickness occurs in early pregnancy up to three months. The expectant mother should take usual diet. Small and frequent (6–7 times) well-spaced meals, rather than 2–3 large meals, are better. Before getting up out of bed in the morning, eating 2–3 biscuits helps to reduce morning sickness. In addition getting up slowly from the bed may help. Avoiding excess of tea and coffee or artificial drinks helps in morning sickness. Use of ginger has been suggested to be effective.

Which diet should be taken in hypertension – During high blood pressure in pregnancy, the salt intake should be restricted. (less than 5 g/day). Pickles and sauces contain lot of salts and should be avoided. It is advisable to avoid fried and fatty food also.

Diet for diabetes mellitus during pregnancy – The diabetic mother should take about 1800 cal. /day. The two basic principles are low caloric diet and maintenance of weight. The diet should be low in refined and high in roughage and fibres. Foods that are high in sugar and glucose are to be avoided. Foods like biscuits, bread rolls, cereals, porridge, potatoes, dried fruits, milk, cheese, meat, thick soups are to be taken in moderation. Food items which can be eaten as desired are green vegetables, clear soups, meat extracts, tomatoes, lemon and light tea. Daily requirement should be planned as carbohydrates, 210 gm. (1050 cal.) 2/3 pints of milk (260 cal.)/(370 ml) Proteins (280 cal.) fats (220 cal.) = total 1810 cal. It should be in 3 main meals and 3 snacks times. Nibbling of food rather than gorging will slow the carbohydrate absorption.

6. 16. Exercise and mental well being

Both, exercise and rest are essential to keep fit and to have an easy delivery for pregnant women. Exercise depends on the routine work of the mother. If she does all the household chores, then simple walk, either in the morning or in the evening is required. If she sits most of the day, it is good to do mild to moderate exercises (warm-ups, arms movements and stretching, lying down movements of legs) and walk. Psychological preparation of the mother and exercises should be started from 4th month onwards. Breathing exercises, maintenance of correct posture and perineal exercises are also advisable. In pregnancy there are mood swings due hormonal changes leading to anger and irritability. Pregnant women should be mentally relaxed and happy without apprehensions. She should read informative books and should also keep herself busy and relaxed by taking care of plants, flowers and by practicing meditation. Exercise helps in controlling blood pressure, reduces stress, tones the muscles, feeling of physical well being and makes the delivery easy.

Warming up – The warm up exercises are arms movement and stretching up legs movements and moderate intensity of walking. These are the starter of other exercises. Ten minutes of warming up exercise should be done before aerobic exercise.

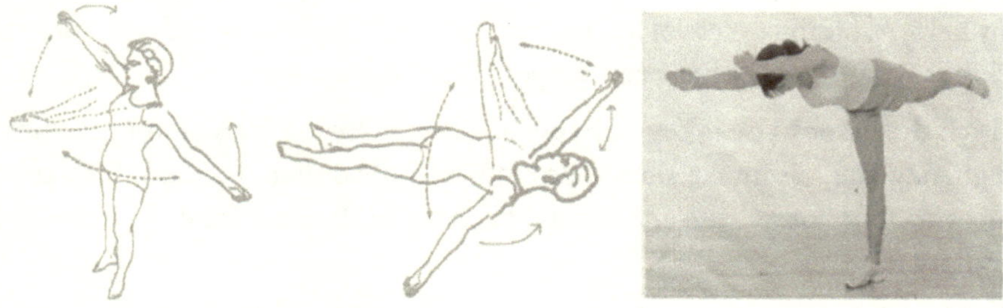

Warming up

Exercises useful during pregnancy – Four types of exercises are helpful in pregnancy.

1. **Aerobic**

2. **Yoga**

3. **Pelvic and abdominal toning**

4. **Relaxation**

Aerobic exercises – These exercises stimulate body circulation by increasing the heart rate and respiratory rate, and thus oxygenation of the expectant mother and the baby. Increased muscle tone and strength are helpful in weight bearing of the baby. These also help in reducing weight in cases of obese mothers. Not only this, such exercises also relieve backache, constipation, control blood sugar and instill confidence in mother, induce good sleep and relieving anxiety. These exercises include brisk walking, swimming, stationary cycling, however walking is ideal.

Yoga – Certain yogic exercises and pranayam are good for mothers. These involve stretching exercises which increase respiratory capacity. These exercises increase muscle tone and strength, relieve constipation, backache, reduce stress anxiety and provide good sleep, thus help in physical and mental well being. Increase in respiratory capacity helps in oxygenation of the mother and baby. Practice yoga under expert advice.

Pelvic and abdominal toning

(a) Abdominal breathing: Lie on the floor with knees bent to about 45° and sole of the feet resting on floor. Inhale. Draw your abdomen in and waist up and tighten your buttock muscle, then exhale. 10–15 times.

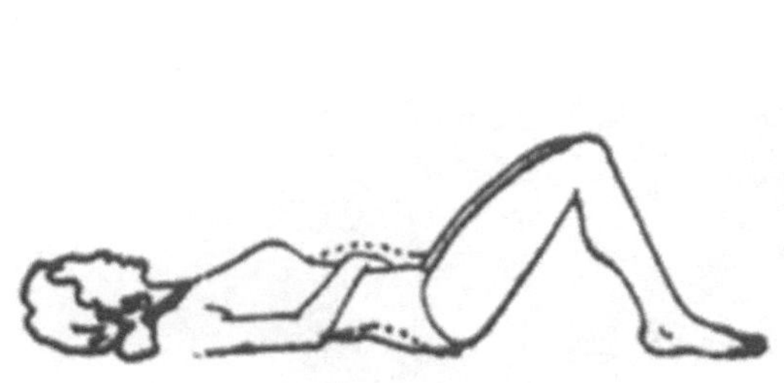

(a) Abdominal Breathing & kegal exercise   **(b) Abdominal Breating-while standing**

The exercise can be performed in standing position also (10–15 tines)

(b) Kegel exercise: Lie on your back with knees bent and soles resting on floor. Draw the muscles of vagina and anus in for 8–10 second than slowly release. Do it frequently during the cay (about 25–30 tines)

(c) Bend the knees and lift your feet up: Rotate your hips to the left and right sides 15–20 times. Keep back of chest touching the ground.

(d) Lie on the back, try to touch your knees with the chin or hug, keep pelvis touching the floor. Practice both knees together and also alternate knees (10–15 times).

(e) Lie on your back with both kneesbent and soles on the floor, try to raise your back above the ground, stay in this position for 5–10 sec. than come to former position. (10–15 times)

(f) Squatting position: Sitting with legs apart in squatting position on your toes for about a minute. 10 times every times 2–3 times/day. This helps in tonic perennial muscle and also for engaging head of the baby if required.

Relaxing

    i.   Lie down on your side with support to your legs/abdomen by a pillow.

    ii. Relaxation can be achieved by sitting with pelvis on the floor, bending knees, keeping soles on the floor and back supported by cushions.

6. 17. Lifestyle

Do's and Don't's for keeping fit: Pregnant women should keep healthy life style for which she is advised as follows:

- Take medical expert advice before exercising.

- Hot baths, sauna bath and steam baths to be avoided.

- Exercise place should be well ventilated and comfortable.

- Wear loose, stretchable clothes for exercise.

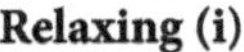
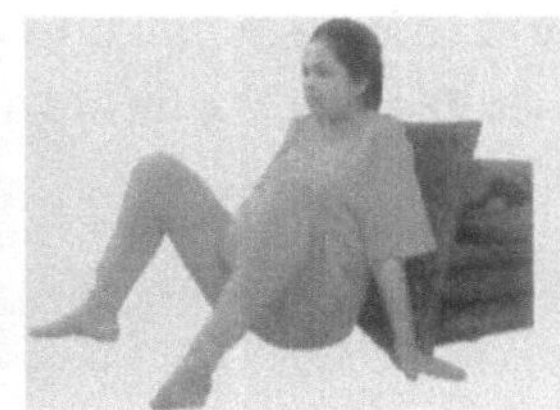

Relaxing (i)   **Relaxing (ii)**

- Exercise for about half an hour every day.

- High risk pregnancies should take great care and do relaxation techniques. Consult your doctor.

- In case of pain and cramps, breathlessness, palpitation or giddiness during or - after, do not continue exercising.

- No lying flat on your back exercises after 4th month of pregnancy

- Avoid exercises in last three months of pregnancy.

- Touch the toes exercise, not advised.

- Do every exercise in moderation, do not do strenuous exercises.

- Do not exercise while empty stomach, take light snacks.

- Meditation and exercise help body and mind to function normally, leading to easy delivery.

Posture – Bad postures in pregnancy leads to muscle pains and problems in pregnancy.

(a) Sitting – While sitting on a chair, keep back of the chest straight with back supporting chair.

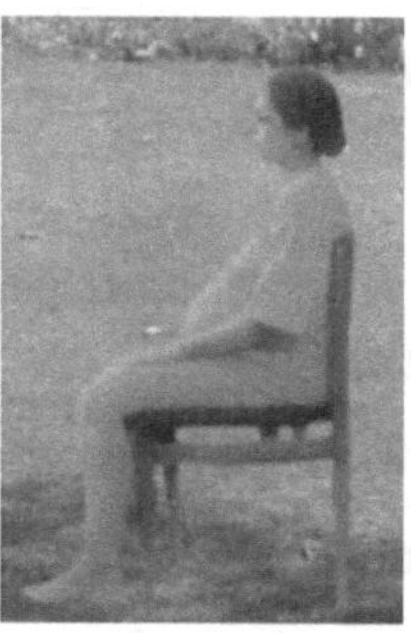

Sitting

(b) Lifting – While lifting small weights, do not bend at waste. First sit on your toes, pick up the things and stand, keeping your back straight.

Lifting

(c) Standing – Since during pregnancy, the weight of uterus and foetus falls in front, the mother tries to lean backwards. Try to correct this posture by standing straight and keeping feet apart.

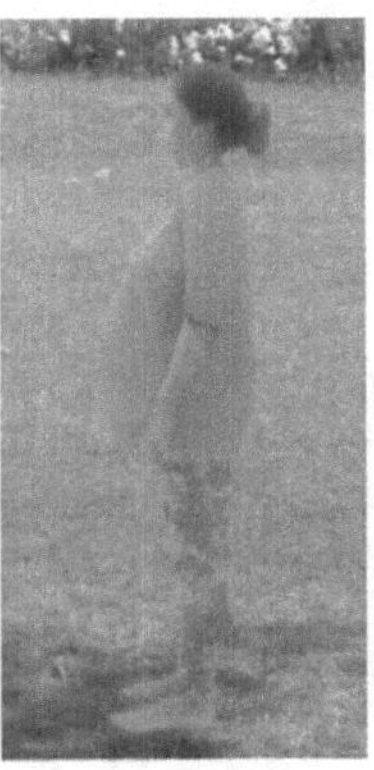

Standing

(d) Lying down (relaxing) – Try to take rest, by lying down on either side with cushion between legs and under the abdomen.

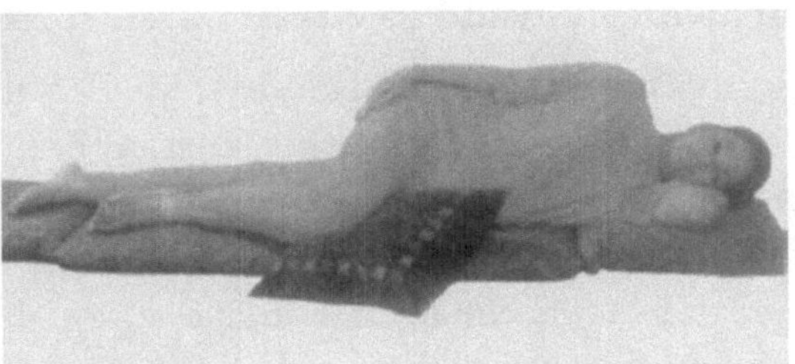

Lying Down

Mental well being – The expectant mother should follow few simple rules to keep herself mentally calmposed.

1. Make home atmosphere congenial.

2. Keep your temperament pleasant.

3. Keep relations harmonious.

4. Healthy discussions.

5. Meditation.

6. Exercise – walking and yoga.

7. Proper diet.

8. Rest and sleep.

9. Creative work and pleasant reading, music, painting and plant care.

Avoid – Watching violence and obscenities on TV, cinema and late sleeping, smoking, alcohol consumption, tea, coffee, soft aerated drinks and drugs.

6. 18. No self medication especially first three months of pregnancy

In 1961 and 1962, a drug known as thalidomide, a mild sedative was given to pregnant women which caused deformed limbs and other malformation in newborn children in Germany and United Kingdom. Millions of such tablets were used in pregnant women. The medical profession got stunned and shocked by the tragedy to thousands of deformed newborns.

We do not know, how many other drugs are causing miscarriage, still birth, malformations and mental retardation. Some of the drugs have been tested in pregnancy, the details are available in textbooks. Some of the drugs have been tested on the foetus but total answer is ethically not possible. Few of them commonly used drugs are listed below with their effects.

6. 19. Maternal medication and its effects on the foetus

Most of the drugs cross the placenta and can adversely affect the foetus. During first 3 months of pregnancy, one should avoid taking any drugs, including iron, vitamins or minerals unless the doctor weighs the medical problem of the mother and potential untoward effects on the foetus. When foetal organs are developing, it is advisable that the mother should always disclose about her pregnancy to the treating physician so that relatively safe drugs are prescribed.

Mother should avoid self medication. She should take medicines under the supervision and advice of the doctor. This is because the drugs can lead to defects in the foetus and newborn brain and other parts of the body.

Drugs/ailments	Effects on foetus and new-born
Anti-thyroid drugs	Hypothyroidism, goiter
Alcohol	Intra-uterine growth retardation (IUGR)
Aspirin	Premature closure of ductus arteriosus
Caffeine	Low birth weight (LBW)
Carbamazepine	Neural tube defects
Cocaine	Abnormal brain development, LBW and IUGR

Drugs/ailments	Effects on foetus and new-born
Chloroquine	Deafness
Cigarette Smoking	L B W
Corticosteroids	Cleft lip and palate, cardiac defects
Tetracylines	Teeth discolouration, growth retardation
Vitamin D	Hypercalcaemia
Phenytoin	Cleft palate, Microcephaly
High Fever	Spinal defect
Rubella	Cardiac defects, blindness, deafness
Progestin	Virilization

There are many other drugs like anti-epileptics, hormones (Oral Contraceptives), anti-cancer and anti-hypertensives which have adverse effects on the unborn child.

Researches were carried out in German mothers about thalidomis. It was reported that this drug when taken by mother between thirty nine and forty one days after menstruation, there was complete absence of arms in the new-born infant, and when taken between forty one to forty four days, absence of legs were also noted. New born infant without ears were also noted in the study. One or two tablets during first three months when the foetus was developing caused the catastrophe.

Animal studies do not be always correlate with the effect on human beings. Every drugs ethically cannot retried on pregnant woman. Drugs in few instance if given to pregnant women causing no noticeable harm, cannot be termed as safe for all pregnant mothers. That is why it is repeatedly advised that pregnant women should not take any drug – not even aspirin or vitamins during first three months of pregnancy without specialist consultation. We agree that millions of woman have taken some kinds of drug during pregnancy and delivered normal babies but why to gamble?

Brain injuries are difficult to detect immediately after birth and it takes repeated examination of children who show delayed milestones and it may take few months to become clear that the child is mentally subnormal and it is more so difficult to pin point the cause of the defect. It may be drug or other factors.

The mother are advised to stop medicines which are being taken before pregnancy, unless doctor advises to continue them. Mothers come to know of pregnancy atleast two weeks after her establishment of pregnancy when she stops to have next periods, when organ formation have already started.

Medicines are likely to have bad effects during these two weeks when she is not aware of pregnancy.

The mother should prefer the natural course of delivery if possible. Too many medicines including anesthesia may sometimes cause problems in unborn child. Avoid any kind of surgery during early pregnancy even dental treatment and inform your doctor about pregnancy, it is a must. We mean by medicine not just tablets but may be injections, local applicants including sprays and ointments, powders, nasal drops, tonics, mineral and vitamins.

Through some of the medicine have been declared safe for mother and unborn child but should be taken under medical supervision, but avoid during first three months of pregnancy. These are as follows:

6. 20. Safe drugs during pregnancy

Topical medicines	Systemic medicines
	Acetaminophen
Benzoyl benzoate lotion	Antacid,
Calamine lotion	Astemizole
Clindamycin	Benzodiazepines
Erythromycin	β – adrenergic receptor antagnist
Local anaesthetics	Bisacodyl
Naphazoline	Calcium
Oxymetazoline	Cephaloporins (see insert)
Phenylephrine	Chlorpromazine
Tritinoin (Vitamin A)	Codeine
Xylometazoline	Cyclizine
Zinc Oxide Cream	Dimenhydrinate
	Diphenhydramine
	Docusate Sodium
	Erythromycin
	Fluoxetine
	Gucocorticoides
	Glycerine
	Heloperidol
	Heparine

Topical medicines	Systemic medicines
	Hydroxyzine
	Hydralazine
	Insulin
	Labetalol
	Lactulose
	Lithium
	Magnesium Hydroxide
	Meclizine
	Mathimazole
	Methyldopa
	Metaclopramide
	Mineral Oil
	Non-steroidal-anti–inflammatory drugs
	Penicillins
	Phenylephrine
	Prazosin
	Propylthiouracil
	Ranitidine
	Sorbitol
	Streptokinase
	Sucralfate

6. 21. Pregnancy and vaccination

Because of some risks, immunization during pregnancy should largely be avoided. Following are some vaccines indicated and some contra – indicated.

Indicated vaccines during pregnancy

- Tetanus texoids, Diphtheria toxoids are safe

- Polio vaccine (Oral), Yellow fever (not in India) If risk of exposure is high.

- Influenza, Hepatitis B are safe but avoid during 1st trimester.

Contra – indicated during pregnancy

- MMR (Mumps, Measles and Rubella)

- Varicella (Chickenpox)

- Inactivated polio vaccine

Breast feeding and vaccination – Breast feeding women may be vaccinated safely. Though live virus in vaccine may replicate in mother but are not secreted in the breast milk.

6. 22. Prevention of injuries during pregnancy

During pregnancy the uterus enlarges into the peritoneal cavity in the abdomen and it grows from 70 g to 1000 gms. The weight of the mother also increases by 12 kg. The centre of gravity of the mother also changes. Hence the chances of injury to mother also increase. Such injury to the pregnant women often presents an emergency and involves mother and her unborn child. It involves multi – disciplinary approaches involving emergency physician/ surgeon, obstretician and child specialist.

The injuries in pregnant women may be physical due to radiation or chemical exposure. About six to seven percent of all pregnant women experience some sort of injury which tend to increase in third trimester (last twelve weeks) when size of uterus and weight of mother increases. Often the injuries may be accidental while travelling or otherwise (aeroplane, car accidents, motorcycle, scooter, cycle, rikshaw and on foot) leading to blunt injuries or penetrating injuries, injuries by fall and domestic violence.

With the result of injuries, pregnant women and foetus, both can be affected, the mother may suffer from shock which may lead to foetal death due to shock, placental displacement or bleeding.

Travel

One can travel during fourth to sixth month of pregnancy, provided it does not tire the mother. Long journey and air travel should be avoided during early and later months of pregnancy. Between 14 to 28 weeks of pregnancy, the morning sickness is no more and the body of the mother is well adjusted to the changes. However, if the pregnancy is high risk (need special care), the journey should be avoided. Avoid small planes, sudden changes in air pressure can cause problems with pregnancy. Avoid travel by motorcycle, scooter, rickshaw and bicycle. Travelling by motorcycle, scooter, rickshaw or bicycle cause jerk, this cause impact over uterus and may cause premature birth or uterus bleeding. Travelling by an automobile causing accident leads to throwing of passenger or driver out and causing impact which can cause rib or bone injury or head and neck injuries.

Internal injuries may cause internal bleeding and shock in which the person becomes pale and pulse becomes feeble and irregular. The unborn also suffers for shock which affects his brain causing death.

Sexual intercourse during pregnancy

It should be avoided during first three months and last two months of pregnancy to prevent risk of abortion and uterine infection. In between, sexual intercourse causes no harm to foetus as the baby is protected by a bag of fluid but this is to be avoided in high risk pregnancies. In normal pregnancy position during intercourse should not put pressure over abdomen. It may be side to side, women on the top or male from behind.

6. 23. Avoid X – Ray radiation exposure

Radiation injuries – The radiation effects the growing tissue of the unborn child, cause death of tissue, genetic mutations, production of cancer cells, a late effect. It damages the sensitive brain of foetus during first three months in uterus. It was seen that some mothers who were accidentally expose to X – ray during abdominal and pelvic diseases gave birth to brain damaged babies. Ionizing radiation, X – ray radiation produce injury in the same manner. Exposure to entire body 100 roentgens usually produce illness in human foetus. Atomic radiation can result in death within hours to days when entire body is exposed. Such radiation cause malaise, fever, nausea, vomiting, diarrhoea, blood changes within one week. Late effects are chromosomal abnormalities, blood cancer, opacities in eye lens, thyroid disease, sterility, skin problems, bone tumours, teeth defects and arrest of growth may occur. Hence the unborn should be protected for x-rays or ionising radiation. Chernobyl diasaster in Russia had taken lives of many women and unborn children.

Avoid x – rays examination or radiation treatment in abdominal area during first three months of pregnancy.

6. 24. Be aware of chemical injuries

The chemical are increasingly invading our environment which are causing damage to foetus and the child.

The pollutants are present in water air and food. Methyl mercury in 1950 caused an epidemic of brain injuries (cerebral palsy) due to contamination of fish by waste dumped at bay in Japan by a factory. In 1968, there was an epidemic due contamination of cooking oil by polychlorinated biphenyls (PCB). The pregnant women gave birth to premature and small new born infants as compared to gestational period.

Eleven of the fifteen children were born in a Hungarian village with birth defects. The mothers had eaten fish treated with trichlorfon, an insecticide. Lead is present in paints and colours. Air borne lead in vehicles smoke and dust causes mental symptoms in children.

Anesthesia and pain relieving drugs affect the foetus as well as mother. Since these drugs reduce the oxygen supply to the mother due to decrease in their respiratory rate, hence affect the foetus. Drugs in mother make foetus depressed whose crying and breathing may be delayed and may remain somewhat inactive.

6. 25. Avoid cigarette smoking

The pregnant woman who smoke heavily are likely to give birth to low weight children. Babies born to smoker mother are about 200 gms less in birth weight than average newborns and also shorter in length. Their overall growth is retarded. This is due to nicotine present in tobacco which crosses to foetus through placenta in smoker mothers. High level of carbon monoxide in the smoke reduced oxygen in foetus. This affects the brain of the newborn. Such children found difficulties in school learning also. Hence smoking during pregnancy should be avoided.

6. 26. Alcohol and narcotics

The pregnant women who use alcohol or narcotic drugs are at high risk. There is higher incidence of sexually transmitted and other diseases including AIDS, hepatitis, toxemia, premature rupture of membranes, breech delivery, hence adversely affect the child during birth as well as before birth. The children are often small for their dates and premature. It also affect short term memory of the child later on as it depresses the brain. Foetal Alcohol syndrome includes growth retardation, facial abnormalities, heart defect, joint abnormalities and mental deficiency.

Heroin – Heroin addiction in mothers causes malnutrition and delivery of low birth weight children. Malnutrition of the mother has bad effects on the foetus.

Still births are also common. The new born may be irritable, rigid and may have fits.

Cocaine – Cocaine addiction in mothers cause premature delivery, foetal asphyxia, small head of infant, bleeding in infant brain and sudden death of the child.

6. 27. Prevent prematurity

Premature literally means immaturity to newborn delivered before 37 weeks is called premature. Previously, prematurity was defined by weightless then 2500 grams at birth, but now it is called low birth weight (LBW). Such children may be premature or small for their gestational age (SGA) or both. Such children are associated with high morbidity and mortality. About 7–8% births are premature. Small for gestational age are due to intrauterine growth retardation (IUGR), low socioeconomic status, malnutrition, anaemia, inadequate prenatal maternal care, chromic illness, drug addiction, placental problem, close spacing of pregnancies, mother having more than four children. Premature infants, who are low birth weight and appropriate for gestational age in general are due to inability of uterus to hold the baby for full term, while Intrauterine growth retardation is due to poor efficiency of placenta or growth of foetus.

Such children require extra care such as frequent feeding, protection from infection, and control of temperature. They respond badly to over medication and oxygen. Premature may show lag in IQ. They may be of around 90 points. Many learning difficulties and may suffer from mental problem later in life. Their intelligence as a whole is slightly lower than normal. The children with less than 2000 grams weight at birth are not found to be of superior IQ. The children with even lower weight may suffer from spasticity, mental retardation, Speech and hearing difficulties, visual and behavioural problems.

6. 28. Avoid exposure to contagious diseases during pregnancy

Illness in mother during pregnancy can cause birth defects or mental retardation in child or it may terminate in miscarriages. Such infections are often viral in origin. Contagious diseases are infections which spread to person by direct contact. When a pregnant women has illness with fever, the women is evaluated for infections. The common infections were thought to be TORCH. An acronym which stands for TO = Toxoplasmosis, R = Rubella (german measles), C = Cytomegalovirus and H = Herpes virus. Subsequently word S was added to it making the acronym STORCH. S stands for Syphilis. But now two other diseases, viral infection such as parvovirus and varicella–zoster. (VZV) has been added to the acronym. Recently AIDS and Hepatitis B have become cause of infection in mother and foetus. These infections cause disease in both, foetus and newborn. The Process of multiplication of infectious agent continues in pregnant mother after she gets infected. During this time placenta gets involves and infection spreads in foetus causing damage to various organs and a malformed baby is born.

The mother who has influenza during early pregnancy runs the risk of baby having birth defects and later learning difficulties. Influenza vaccines can be given to pregnant woman in case of influenza outbreak to protect her from infection.

a. **Cytomegalovirus** is one the most common cause of congenital infection causing malformation in newborn. It causes intrauterine growth retardation, jaundice, bleeding disorder, small heads, brain calcification and mental abnormalities, eyes involvement and deafness. The diagnosis is made by culturing amniotic fluid obtained during amniocentesis, when diagnosis is being made in unborn child, but after birth, isolation of virus can be made from urine and saliva of infected new born. In adult, the disease is mild that there may be no symptoms. Pregnant woman's blood is tested for infections. Hygienic measures such as good hand washing and avoidance of contact with oral secretions should be undertaken. There no efficacious vaccine available.

b. **Herpes infection** – It causes fever, blisters, cold sores and genital infection. During Pregnancy of woman, this infection spreads to foetus and causes pre maturity and death of unborn or it may cause brain, eyes, skin involvement. Brain involvement reduces the head size and brain atrophy. Eye involvement is in the form of retina problems and small eyes. The disease is diagnose by placental cord blood samples in unborn child in which virus or DNA may be estimated but in new born child secretions of eye, urine, skin and trachea can be taken for investigation.

The disease can be prevented in newborn from genital infection of the mother by doing delivery by Cesaren section or giving protective medicine.

c. **Varicella** – Zoster virus leads to chickenpox or Herper zoster. Intrauterine infection causes serious problems when pregnant women contacts chicken pox, the foetus also gets infected. German studies have been made which reveal that congenital varicella syndrome causes eye involvement in the form of small eyes, retina involvement, cataract, brain damage small head, brain calcification and damage to spinal cord leading to malformed extremities. The prevention of disease is made by an administration of immune globulin.

d. **German Measles** – German measles has almost been eliminated due to regular universal vaccination but before vaccination it was a leading cause of epidermic which caused intrauterine growth retardation, cataract and small eye and many other problems, such as skin rash. The victim of disease can spread the virus about a week before the development of skin rash. Cervical gland enlargement and catarrhal symptoms also occur.

e. **Parvovirus** – In 1975, Parvovirus was first isolated and disease cause by it is known as Erythema infectious. Usually the infection occurs in teenagers but also may cause disease in adults. Pregnant women if infected, complains of fever, sore throat, joint pain and skin rash, spontaneous abortion may result. Foetal manifestation are swelling of the body and heart failure. There is no vaccine available for prevention of the disease nor specific medicine available.

f. **Human Immune Deficiency Virus (HIV)** – The virus causes AIDS (acquired immune deficiency syndrome) the disease nearly always acquired, infects the newborn from infected mother. The pregnant gets the disease through unsafe sex, contaminated blood transfusion or through intravenous contaminated syringes. The drug users sharing needle with HIV infected persons. The transmission of disease to foetus depends upon severity of disease. It may be 25–70%. It is one of the major problem in India, Africa and Thailand. The virus is present in breast milk hence mother should not give breast milk to new born. The disease reduces the capacity of fighting infection in body. Infected infant manifests much later when chronic problems of diarrhoea, failure to thrive, weakness or oral thrust is seen in infants. The disease is diagnosed by blood testing. Drug prevention is partially successful.

g. **Syphilis** – Syphilis is caused by a germ spirochete. The infection spreads by sexual contact. In the mother the germ infects the foetus through placenta. Forty percent of deaths occur in affected foetuses.

It involves liver, causing jaundice, enlargement of lymph nodes, bone involvement and skin involvement, teeth and brain involvement also occurs. Antibiotic are given for treatment. Avoid unsafe sex.

h. **Taxoplasmosis** – Taxoplasmosis is an acquired diseases caused by taxoplasma, a protozoan and spreads by infected cats through their farces. The food material which is contaminated by cat's farces such as raw meat or other food material is eaten by human which causes the disease. It does not spread by human to human except through placenta to foetus. 50% of infected pregnant women, transmit the disease to foetus. The infection causes premature delivery, jaundice, enlarged head size, eye involvement and brain calcifications, there by mental retardation and fits.

Medication can prevent infection of foetus by sixty percent if given to infected pregnant woman. No protective vaccine is available. The disease can be prevented by using well done meat, egg or milk. The cats should be kept indoor maintained on prepared diet. Avoid contacting the cats. Wash the edibles and hands, kitchen surfaces thoroughly. Identify infected foetus and treating him.

i. **Hepatitis B** – Hepatitis B virus (HBV) highly infectious, carried throughout life, Spreads from infected blood transfusion, contaminated needle, tattoing, unsafe sexual intercourse and mother to foetus, Hepatitis B vaccine is available. Blood test detects positive Australia antigen. Hepatitis B can cause lives failure, coma and chromic. Hepatitis which can be fatal. Infants of infected mothers may initially be asymptomatic but are at high risk in later life. They should routinely be vaccinated against hepatitis B from birth onwards.

Some of the diseases in mother could be prevented through vaccination during pregnancy and before conception which is as under.

Vaccination in pregnancy, breast feeding and immune compromised states.

Immunization of pregnant woman is basically avoided. Pregnant woman can safely be given tetanus and diphtheria toxoids. Live vaccines should not be given during pregnancy except polio and yellow fever (not in India) vaccines if the risks are high. Inactivated vaccines such as influenza and hepatitis B are safe in pregnant woman.

Nursing mothers may be given vaccination safely. Most of the vaccines are not excreted in breast Milk.

Live attenuated vaccines are contraindicated in immune compromised patients. However, for passive immunization, immunoglobulin may be used.

Vaccination for Travelling

Different countries may require certain specific vaccines, along with routine vaccination for the entry. Make it sure before you travel.

6. 29. Know your and your husband's blood group for incompatibility

Human blood has been found to posses many types of factors. Two of them are very prominent. Rh and ABO which are accepted every where. We shall first describe. Rh problem as below – The individuals are designated Rh$^+$ (positive) if this factor is present in the blood and if factor is absent, they are called Rh$^-$. This factors is governed by Rh genes (dominant recessive) in human and is present in 85% of population. The Rh type produces number of blood group factors (Cc, Dd, Ee). It was found that when Rh$^+$ (positive) blood was injected into a person with Rh$^-$ (negative) blood, Rh antibodies were formed which caused breaking of blood cells in Rh$^+$. Rh (D) immune globulin was prepared from blood of Rh antibodies which when injected into Rh negative mother after delivery of Rh positive infant, prevent this breaking of blood. D antigen of Rh group is present in 90% of Rh$^+$positive mothers and is responsible for blood incompatibility. This incompatibility can be prevented by giving injection anti-D to the mother.

When Rh$^-$ women during pregnancy has Rh$^+$ infant (father being Rh$^+$) during first delivery or abortion, small amount of blood of Rh$^+$ infant enters into the mother's circulation, antibodies are formed against D antigen of infant in the mother. In next pregnancy these antibodies enter into Rh$^+$ foetus and breaks the blood of infant leading to anemia jaundice or infants death. This is called hemolytic disease of newborn.

6. 30. Asphyxia – effects on foetus

Asphyxia (lack of intake of oxygen) is measure of infant morbidity and mortality which cause cerebral palsy, mental retardation or lung problems. The brain damage is usually noticed after a long time when the child is unable to develop normal milestones. Baby's supply of oxygen is cut down markedly even during natural birth. Anesthesia, and drugs given to the mother further cut down baby's oxygen during labour, may result in newborn brain damage or even death. The effects of muscle relaxants, pain relievers, depressants, given to mother during labour, can cause difficulties in establishing respiration in the newly born. Because of their low margin of safety if given at wrong time during labour, Their effects would depressed the child. This decision of drug administration depends on the doctor's skill and knowledge. The mother should co-operate with doctor orders, however the mother should know about when to go to hospital?, about the labour and control of labour pains along with certain queries to make her comfortable which will psychologically help her to co-operate with doctors. She should be aware of the scoring in newborn done (APGAR SCORE) after the delivery, for need of child's resuscitation. Some knowledge of assisted delivery, caesarean section and abnormal delivery shall make her more wiser.

6. 31. Hypothyroidism

Thyroid hormone deficiency in mother may lead to thyroid deficiency in newborn, which effects the brain adversely. In mother, thyroid gland may be involved due to drug, iodine deficiency or disease, which should be treated adequately.

6. 32. Get mother and baby checked for phenyketonuria (PKU)

Phenylalanine is an essential amino acid. Phenylalanine is not utilized in some patient for protein systhesis due to deficiency of an enzyme called phenylalanine hydroxylase and its level increases in the blood and cause manifestation and pass into urine. Pregnant women with phenylkatonuria (PKU) who are not on low phenylalanine diet have higher risk of spontaneous abortions. Infants born to such mothers are likely to have mental retardation, small sized head and heart problems. These complications are due to high levels of phenylalanine in mother's blood. The access amount of phenylalanine is excreted in urine.

Mothers tobe, are advised to start on low phenylalanine diet before conception to keep phenylalanine levels low throughout pregnancy. Excess of phenylalanine disrupts the normal metabolism of the mother. The affected children appear to be normal at birth but mental retardation gradually develops in few months to bring IQ of children 50 points lower by the first year when they start taking normal diet. The children become hyperactive have, abnormal movement and have speech defect. Infants are blonder and have fair skin and blue eyes and learn to walk much later but life expectancy may be normal. The disease is inherited from parents who may not have the symptoms of the disease because it is carried by recessive genes by each of parents. The chances of having the disease by child is one in four.

To save the child from such complication (PKU), the child should be investigated and treated during first weeks of life and placed on low phenylalanine diet for several years. The rigid control may be relaxed after 6 years of age but some control in necessary. The diagnosis is made by testingurine as well as blood.

Baby Care After Birth

Neil was a gifted child, he used to walk with ease and talked2–3 word sentence at one and a half years of age. After some time he became ill and during that illness, he became unconscious and started having fits. After treatment he regained consciousness, his fits stopped but he was not of the same behavior, walking and talking wise. Because he had developed meningitis.

A new born baby, few days after birth had developed jaundice, his cry was hoarse and he was lethargic and not active during wakeful time. Even after few years he remained short statured, had low mental faculties and had delayed mile stones. His blood tests revealed deficiency of thyroid hormone. When he grew up, his intelligence remained subnormal even with the treatment. He was suffering from thyroid deficiency, we called such a child a cretin.

A newborn few hours old weighing more than 4 kg had fits. Mother was diabetic. Her disease persisted throughout pregnancy as well. The child was dozy and pale. The blood of the newborn was tested which showed low blood sugar. He was given glucose for the treatment. Such children do have guarded intelligence depending upon prolongation, severity and recurrence of low blood sugar. The mother should have been treated well for her diabetes mellitus in the very beginning.

The child intellectual ability depends upon the – 1) inherited quality of brain 2) damage caused by the disease process and 3) interaction with the environment. One cannot change the heredity in i. e. quality of the brain matter of the child because this is determined by the genes which he possesses, which he received from mother and father. The damage by disease depends upon the part of brain involved. It may be general senses or special senses or motor activity paralysis which one has to revitalize by physiotherapy and medicines. The third factor is interaction with the environment and shall be discussed elsewhere in details which is very important for acquiring intelligence.

Few children are unable to concentrate over one particular thing, have trouble with learning and are overactive, poorly coordinated with perception difficulties. Such children are called minimal brain dysfunction syndrome which is difficult to detect by routine tests. But general examination and behavior reveals that he is below the age of his equivalent child which indicate some type of brain damage. Such children are not able to apply their mental capacity for proper learning, suffer from behaviour problems and they became emotional too.

Many causes of the mental retardation are preventable. There are certain known ways, the parents can learn and follow. They can guard the physical health of the child from diseases and injuries. Following are some important ways of protection.

7. 1. Skilled care for your child (also chapter 2)

We have already discussed that the child should be protected from various infections and diseases before birth so that the child is born with normal growing brain.

The child needs to be protected at the time of his birth, for which services of a skilled obstetrician and gynecologist are required who can diagnose and control the maternal diseases. Intrauterine malnutrition, premature delivery, placental insufficiency, toxins such as alcohol, cocaine, smoking and infections like human immune deficiency virus, toxoplasma, cytomegalovirus could be avoided. While for delivery of the child, lots of skills are required to avoid brain injury, bleeding inside the child's brain, delayed and difficult labour, administration of antibiotic to the newborn if the mother had leaking membranes for more than 24 hrs to avoid neonatal septicemia.

A layman is unable to understand the hazard of labour hence it is important that the delivery of the mother is conducted by a specialist doctor. Preventive vaccination to the mother such as tetanus, Poliomytites, influenza, hepatitis should be given but not during first three months of pregnancy. Before conception, the women should be vaccinated for mumps, measles rubella, and chicken pox. The family should take initiative to take measure for child care. If the mother has the history of receiving such anti-thyroid drugs, the child after birth any develop hypothyroidism which should be kept in mind. Similarly child of diabetic mother need lot of care to prevent low sugar which may adversely affect his brain.

7. 2. Brain insult after birth

Dr. Andelman of Chicago, Board of health was of the openion that the disease even in mild form during delivery and after birth may play a significant role in causation of mental retardation, learning difficulties, behavior problems and personality. The brain insult around birth may be due to (a) infection (b) injury (severe head injury) (c) suffocation, insufficient oxygenation (asphyxia), difficult and prolonged cessation of breathing (d) Toxins such as lead (e) Metabolic diseases such as low blood sugar levels in the blood. Bleeding inside the brain (intracramial hemorrhage) (f) malnutrition.

It has been estimated that approximately 80–90% of the population fall within mid-range 70–80 points of IQ. While 5% fall between severe to profound retardation.

(a) Infections

Infections are a frequent causes of children diseases. Approximately 10% of the infants are infected during delivery or first month of life. They acquire infection just before or during delivery from the mother. Ecoli, chlamydia, mycoplasma, herpes are the few examples.

Infections of amniotic fluid in which infants is bathed in uterus, can get affected if amniotic fluid leaks for more than twenty four hours before delivery or mother has an infection or the delivery is difficult one.

Premature babies or low birth weight neonates are greatly predisposed to infections during resuscitation at birth and exchange blood transfusion. Hospital acquired infections, hospital personnels, inanimate sources (contaminated equipment's), family contacts are also various sources of infection. Infection spreads to blood of the infants and this infection goes to brain causing mental retardation. The infected child suffers from fever, drowsiness bluish discolouration, loose motions and vomiting, inability to feed & shrill cry, unconsciousness and fits. Medication and antibiotic before delivery, rapid delivery of newborn infant, scrubbing of hands, isolation of infant, cord care equipment sterilization are essential for effective prevention of infection.

Later on also various infection, may it be bacterial such as septic and tuberculer meningitis, haemophilus influenza type B, protozoal such as cerebral malaria, toxoplasmosis or it may be viral infection such as influenza, chickenpox, measles and cytomegalovirus are often the causes of infection, are also cause of brain insult and lead to brain damage.

In the past measles and chicken pox were quite prevalent. Many a times these also leave brain damage, resulting in learning and behavioural problems in children. EEG changes may show changes in the brain without any symptoms in the child or minimal brain damage. Such children may develop epileptic fits also. Now a days, the prevalence of measles and chicken pox is much less because of available vaccines. Vaccination is also available for influenza and haemophilus type b. A vaccination schedule is given below for the parent to prevent various preventable infections.

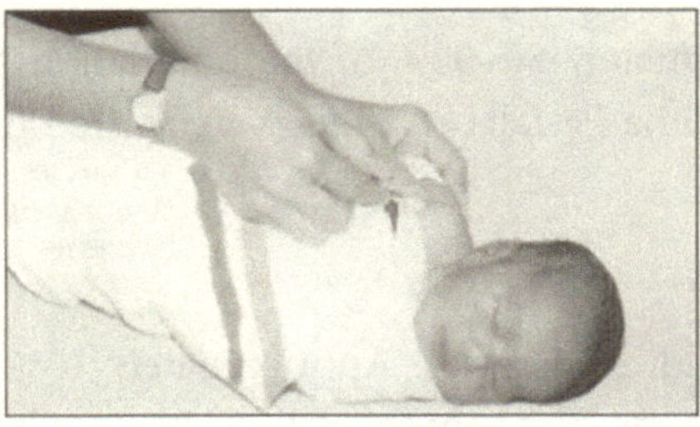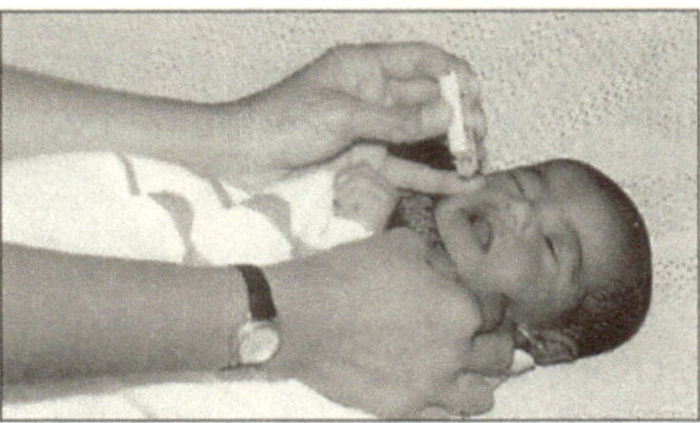

Immunization

b) Immunization schedule

Age	Vaccine
BIRTH	BCG
	OPV-1
	HEP-B-1
6 Wks (1 ½ m)	DTP-1
	OPV-II
	HIB-I
	HEP-B-II
	Rotavirus
	Vit A – I
	Pneumococcal
10 Wks (2 ½ m)	DTP-II
	OPV-III
	HIB-II
	Rotavirus
	Vit A – II
	Pneumococcal

Age	Vaccine
14 Wks (2 ½ m)	DTP-III OPV-IV HIB-III Pneumococcal
6 m	HEP-B-III OPV + Vit. A III – HIB III OPV
9 m	Measles
12 m	HEP-A-I Varicella (Chicken pox)
15 m	MMR, HIB-booster, Polio, DPT, Pneumococcal
18 m	Hepatitis A2
24 m	MN/Influenza – I Typhoid, Pneumococcal
4 Yrs	DTP + OPV – Booster II Infl. Every year Typhoid, Varicella MN-booster
7 Yrs	Typhoid
9–10 Yrs	DT, Typhoid
12 Yrs	MMR Booster Influenza – once a year Typhoid Vac. Every 3 yrs interval

HEP = Hepatitis, DTP = Dephtheria, tetanus, pertussis, DT = Dephtheria, Tetanus

OPV = Oral Polio Vaccine, MMR = mumps, measles, rubella

MN = Menengitis, HIB = Haemophilus Influenza B

Infl = Influenza

c) Effects of vaccination

The vaccination is usually safe and effective but sometimes it is associated with adverse reactions. The most common allergen is egg proteins, the vaccine prepared in egg such as measles, mumps and influenza. Local pain and little swelling or fever occurs with diphtheria, tetanus and antirabies also.

Vaccination			
Vaccine	**Description**	**Primary Vac**	**Boostervac**
BCG	This is against tuberculosis. It is given intradermally on left upper arm. It leaves a mark on the site of injection.	Soon after birth	—
D. P. T. (or DTP) (Diphtheria + Pertussis + Tetanus)	Diphtheria-toxoid Petussis (Whoopingcough) – killed, inactivated bacteria. Tetanus-detoxified exotoxins. Injection are given deep intramuscular, 0.5 ml. Started at 6 weeks of age. Three doses are given at 6–8 weeksinterval. Mild fever, pain or swelling at site of injection results for 24 hours.	6 weeks 10 weeks 14 weeks	1 ¼ yrs, 4 yrs, 10 yr (DT) adult formulation Pertussis not recommended after 6 years DT Adult Formulation every 10 years interval.
Polio Vaccine (OPV)	Oral, trivalent, live attenuated virus vaccine, 2 frops given orally	Birth (5 doses are 4–8 weeks interval	6 m, 1 ¼, yrs, 4 yrs
Tetanus toxoid	Intramuscular Injection	(as given in DPT)	10 yrs, 15 yrs
Measles vaccine	Live attenuated viral Vac.	9 months	
MMR vaccine	Mumps, Measles, Rubella Intramuscular injection, live attenuated virus Vaccine Adverse reactions are rare.	15 months	10–12 yrs
Typhoid vaccine Vi-antigen	0.5 ml intramuscular, local adverse reaction Vi capsular polysaccharide	2–3 yrs	6–7 yrs. 10–12 yrs. Every 3 yrs.
Oral Typhoid Vaccine	Also oral live attenuated capsules given. Empty stomach on alternate days for 3 days after age of 6 yrs of age then every 3 yrs interval.	6 yrs	Every 3 yrs.

Vaccination			
Vaccine	**Description**	**Primary Vac**	**Boostervac**
Hepatitis B Vaccine	Inactivated virus vaccine, recombinant 0.5 ml for hepatitis B disease prevention	Birth, 1 month, 6 months	
Hib Vaccine	For H. influenza type B infection, Injection IM	2 m, 4 m, 6 m or be combined with DPT	15 months 1 dose
Hepatitis A Vaccine	Injection 0.5 ml, against hepatitis A mild adverse reactions (given 1 to 18 years).	One dose at one year One dose after six months	Between 6–12 months of primary.
Rabies	1. Rabies vaccine against rabid dog bite diseases. (1) Human diploid cell antirabies vaccine (HDCV) (2) Purified chick embryo cell rabies vaccine (PCEC) (3) Purified vero cell rabies vaccine (PVRV), mild side effects (4) Anti-rabies serum (a) Human rabies immunoglobulin (20 IU/Kg) (b) Horse serum (40I. U. / Kg)	Pre exposure 0, 7, 28 days (0.1 ml) or Post exposure (1 ml) 0, 3, 7, 14, 28, 90 days in unimmunized or 1 ml 0–3 days in vaccinated Same Same Given in unvaccinated Half dose into wound & half intramuscular	
Varicella	Chicken pox vaccine	At one year	4–5 yrs
Meningococcal Meningitis	Bivalent vaccine, sero group, A, C, injection 0.5 ml subcutaneous	Before 4 yrs.	After 2–3 yrs. of primary vaccine
Influenza	0.25 ml at 2 year/3 years Inactivated (before 10 years of age), 0.5 ml after 10 years of age	2 yrs./3 yrs.	Every year
Pneumococcal vaccine	Capsular Material, Inj.	6, 10, 14 weeks	15 m & 2 yrs

i.   **Live attenuated vaccine:** Measles, Mumps, Rubella (MMR), B. C. G, Poliomyelitis, Typhoid (Oral), Influenza, yellow fever.

ii. **Killed or inactivated:** Petussis, HIB, Typhoid, Hepatitis B, Meningococcal Meningitis, Poliomyelitis, Influenza, Cholera, Rabies Hepatitis A, Pneumococcal, Plague, Japanese Encephalitis

iii. **Toxoid** – Diphtheria and Tetanus

(d) Injuries

Birth injury-while delivery or instrumentation can lead to head injury. Fracture of skull may occurs to cause brain symptoms requiring treatment. At later stage injuries during cycling, games, falling down at stairs, accidents may cause brain injury and are responsible for mental retardation. Head injuries may cause unconsciousness or fits.

With the fore sight, all accidental injuries could be prevented. Here are some tips for the parent to follow to prevent injuries.

Accident implies an event occurring by chance without any prediction or pattern. The understanding has been made to know about risk factors and injuries and develop the programme for prevention and control. All accidents do not result in deaths but may disfigure or cripple the child and shall be uneconomical and consuming lot of time as well. During adolescence or later teen age, most of accidents occur outdoors by vehicles, drowning, sports and burns. At the age of 5–9 years, pedestrian or bicycle injuries are most common: Falls, burns and fire smoke causing asphyxia, choking due to food items, small balls and balloons, homicide, poisoning due to medicines and house hold products and blunt injuries occur in young children and infants more frequently.

Efforts to control injuries include education of parents for safe use and storage of chemicals and medicines, purchase of safe toys, change in product and modification of environment, careful supervision specially in situations of family get together.

Baby – proofing your home

- All the children learn by playing and imitating, pulling-pushing, touching, seeing, hearing and climbing. By doing such manoeuvres they are likely to get injured. Hence make your house safe for children.

- Remove or fix any pavement or foot board that is not level.

- Check base boards for wooden splinters.

- Make all doors and drawers safe. Put baby-proof latches on cabinets and drawers. Put doors on stair-case at both levels.

- Remove table cloth for some time. The child may pull it and things on that table, by coming down, may injure the child. Never put hot dishes or tea pot on the edge of the table as the child may get burn injury.

- Do not put pillows in the crib to avoid baby's suffocation.

- Make sure that bedding and curtains are atleast three feet away from electrical points.

- All power electrical points should be properly covered and secured.

- Do not put mobile or other phone near the crib as baby may get disturbed all the time when bell rings or wires may be pulled-up by the child and he gets injured.

- Do not smoke in child's room or near the child.

- Plastic bags, cigarette butts should be disposed off properly. Choking by plastic bags is not rare.

- Do not keep anything smaller than the baby's fist such as nuts, berries, resins, toffees, etc. within the reach of the child or he may be choked by putting these things in his mouth.

- Keep all sharp objects like knife, scissors, blades, needles and pins out of reach.

- Put all medicines, toxic substances, kerosene, match boxes, burning candles and lamps etc. secured away from the child. The child is in the habit of putting everything into the mouth, so he is likely to have poisoning.

- Keep all the potted plants out of reach of the child, so that he may not eat part of the plant or mud from the pot.

- Keep bathroom close and keep water filled bath tubs or bucket in bathroom or kitchen to avoid drowning.

- The toys should not have pointed or sharp edges.

- Do not allow the child to play with arrows and bows or gulel. (catapult).

- Windows should have grills with bars not more than four inches apart or baby may get fall through.

- No smoke should be created in the house as the baby is likely to get asphyxiated. Allow fresh air to enter in to the house.

- Fire extinguisher may be kept handy for use if small fire breaks out.

- Child should not play alone with fire crackers, some adult person should accompany him.

Do not keep car engine running with garage doors closed. Exhaust contains Carbon monoxide gas which is tasteless, and without smell and very toxic.

- Keep phone numbers of poison centre, hospital, fire station and ambulance handy or depicted clearly near telephone table.

Outdoor protection

Never let a child play on roads with heavy traffic, use parks for playing. Keep the child fully dressed to avoid mosquitoes bites.

- Never let the child swim without adult supervision.

- If the child rides a bicycle, he must use helmet and knee caps.

- Never let a child drive a car or a scooter or such vehicle without "license" since driving between age of 15–17 years have twice the rate of accidents.

- Chest belts and child locks are provided in the car and should be used.

Cuts, lacerations and falls

Cuts are caused by sharp objects like knives, blades, scissors, sharp edged toys, while lacerated wounds are caused by baby-walker, bicycle and fall.

If the wound is small, clean it with soap and water and put Band-Aid or bandage. Small bleeding can be stopped by putting cotton and pressure for few minutes. If wound is larger, consult your doctor. It might require stitching and pressure bandage, antibiotics and also tetanus injection. If there is simple small blood collection without external skin injury, ice pack may be applied. If there is **fracture of bone** or a large swelling and pain, the child should be taken to a specialists doctor who may advise the x-rays.

In case of head injuries, if the child loses consciousness, vomits, or has fits, bleeding from nose, or ears or has head ache, the child should be taken to hospital immediately. Sleep medicines should never be given under such circumstances. Helmets should be used to prevent head injuries while driving bicycle.

(e) Burns

Burns and scalding results from geyser water, spilling of hot tea, milk or hot water or burning candles, burning stove, matchbox or lighting crackers.

Burns

Synthetic material clothes like nylon catches fire easily. Strong acids used in toilets or strong alkalis like caustic soda or dyes can cause burns. Burnt or a scalded parts should be flooded with cold water. If child's clothes catch fire, the child should be wrapped in blanket or bed sheet, the flame will extinguish. Remove the clothes and consult your doctor. As first aid, wash the burnt area with cold water.

(f) Electrical injuries

The electric current can produce shock and burns. The children are in the habit of putting their fingers in the socket and temper with the switches. Keep the socket closed and discourage the child to temper with switches.

Electrical Injuries

If the child gets electric shock, remove him from the electric source by pushing him away with a dry wood and not by hand, otherwise the person himself would get the shock. Switch off the current. If electric shock is severe, it could be fatal. It can cause severe burns and respiratory arrest. Rush to the hospital. He may require resuscitation and intravenous fluids.

(g) Drowning

After drowning in water, suffocation will occur with or without lung aspiration. Children can drown in canal, open drains, open sewers or rain floods and swimming pools. Small children can drown in bath tubs or water full of buckets. Never leave baby unattended while bathing and do not leave bath tubs and buckets filled with water. Even one inch of water level can suffocate a child. Adults should accompany the child for swimming.

Invert the Child for Water Draining from Respiratory

- If child gets drowned and stops breathing, invert him to drain off the water. Clear the mouth, give him mouth to mouth breathing, closing the nose of the child. Take him to hospital urgently without wasting any time. Keep a watch on pulse and respiration.

(h) Foreign bodies

In mouth – small children are in the habit of putting small objects like button, beads, coins, pins or small glass balls in their mouth.

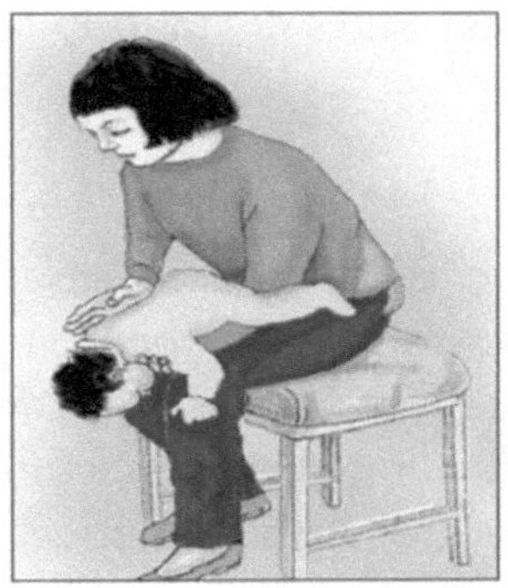

Foreign Body in the Throat

If a child swallows inedible small things, he is likely to pass in stool. Do not force the child to vomit. Keep a track of that thing in stools. X-ray or screening may be required repeatedly to know its position in the intestines.

In ear and nose – small objects in ears or nose should be taken out by a specialist. Attempts to take them out by another person may push them deeper. Do not put oily medicine in to the nose, such medicine may trickle down in to the lungs, and cause pneumonia.

(i) In difficult breathing and asphyxia

A child, while eating some thing (like nuts, seeds, peas or food) starts coughing and feels breathing difficulty, the chances are that some of the material might have gone into throat or wind pipe, due to which child will have difficulty in respiration and there may be cessation of breathing. He may be blue in colour due to lack of oxygen. Insufficient intake of oxygen is also known as Asphyxia. This adversely effects the brain of the child depending upon prolongation of insufficient oxygen. Try to invert the child and thump him at the back so that the object comes out. Take him to hospital if breathing is affected.

In eyes – if an object falls into eyes or there is some chemical injury to the eyes, wash the eye's with clean water, do not rub. Consult an eye specialist.

(j) Nasal bleeding

This usually occurs in childhood and often at night when mother observes the pillow smeared with blood, sometimes in the morning. Often the bleeding is due to a trivial injury around the nose, picking, foreign body or infection in the nose. Make the child sit on chain with the head forwards. Compress the nose for few minutes with fingers. Keep the child quiet. It takes few minute to stop the bleeding. If the above measures do not help consult ear, nose and throat (ENT) specialist.

(k) Suffocation

The child feels difficulty in breathing or feels suffocated due to lack of oxygen. This could be due to smoke by coal, wood burning, or chemicals which produce toxic gases. The coal should be burnt outside the house. Keep the windows and doors open for air exchange. The suffocation can also be caused by children hiding themselves in cupboards, fridge or exposed to car exhaust, cooking gas or by drowning or polythene bags used by child as head mask. Keep polythene bags out of child's reach and fridge and cupboard locked. Rush the child to hospital immediately. Oxygen inhalation or assisted ventilation may be required.

(l) Toxin

Lead poisoning – lead poison is a major health problem which may cause minor to major brain problems. It usually develops slow.

Lead in the body is unnatural and reflects the contamination of the environment. The average blood level should be zero, but often low blood levels of less than 10–15 milligrams % are found in children in survey. The lead is absorbed in the body from contact with vehicular exhaust, paints, prints, lead containing dust through mouth and respiration, old house wall paints, premise of building under renovation, glazed ceramic vessels, lead industry, fumes from burning batteries, cosmetics, leaded gasoline, painted toys and mud eating. The poisoning may be acute or chronic. Symptoms relate to level of lead in the blood. Blackening of gums, behaviour changes, pain in abdomen, vomiting, constipation, fits numbers and even unconsciousness can occur. The encephalopathyis usually at blood levels above hundred milligram percent. The diagnosis is usually made by screening blood levels of suspected patient of lead poisoning. X-rays of long bones show lead lines. If the blood levels are above 10 microgram/dl, parents should be educated for the exposure and levels upto 15 requires the removal of lead source and the matter should be brought to the notice of medical authority. Level above 15 microgram/dl call for drug treatment. For prevention, screening of children should be made starting from 10 to 14 months of age. The house should be completely repainted and made lead free. Lead free petrol is now available in many countries which has helped lessening of lead absorption. Use of gloves, avoiding of inhalation should be practiced at lead industry. Meals for school children should not be wrapped in newsprints papers. Hands should be thoroughly washed before meals. Children should be protected from mud eating.

Other poisoning

In India, kerosene, insecticides, pesticides, polish, paints, thinner, petrol, naphthalene, detergents, perfumes and medicines are mainly responsible for poisoning. Snake bite, bee sting, wasp sting, and scorpion bite can leads to local reaction or shock. The poisoning can lead to local burns, vomiting, unconsciousness, fits or bluish discolouration and fever.

- Keep toxic material or kerosene, paints, medicine etc. at secured place.
- The medicine should be dispensed in child resistant containers.
- Avoid painted toys.
- Give water to the child to drink so that toxic material is diluted in stomach and the action of that material is delayed.
- Make the child vomit by tickling throat or give syrup Ipecac 10–15 ml. by mouth.
- Give activated charcoal (0.5 gm/kg) immediately and repeat the dose every four hours if required. Take the child to hospital urgently.
- Bite sites should be washed and pressure bandage be given proximal to the site for 10–15 minute if the limbs are involved. Take the child to hospital if required. Keep telephone number of poison center handy.

(m) Metabolic disease

Newborn infant of diabetic mother needs special treatment in the hospital.

(n) Cretinism (Hypothyroidism)

Hypothyroidism results from deficient production of thyroid hormones which may be acquired or due to birth defect or thyroid deficiency in mother. The child's weight and length are normal initially after which growth retardation occurs, jaundice may be prolonged. Feeding difficulties and sluggishness, choking spells are common. Constipation, noisy breathing, hoarse cry, subnormal temperature, genital swelling are present. Thyroid screening programme may help to recognize the disease. Thyroid hormone estimation and thyroid stimulating hormone should be tested in the infants blood. Treatment is instituted thereafter.

(o) Bleeding in the brain

Bleeding in the brain may be due to head injury or severe lack of oxygen in the child or bleeding disorders or prolonged or breech deliveries and vitamin k deficiency especially mothers receiving antiepileptic drugs and severely premature infants usually less than 1500 gms at birth.

The bleeding in brain usually occurred during first week of life but may be upto one month of age. The child refuses to take feeds, becomes lethargic, irritable and develops fits. Fontanel becomes buldged. The diagnosis is usually made by computed tomography, ultrasound through anterior fontanel and cerebrospinal fluid examination.

The disease can be prevented by management avoiding birth injuries, administration of low dose indomethacin and vitamin E. Vitamin K should be given routinely to all women receiving anti-epilepsy drugs and to infants after birth.

7. 3. Emergency first aid kit

The emergency kit should be maintained at home and should contain the following things in a box. The box should be handy and easy to carry even while travelling.

- Small roll of cotton
- Six bandages of 2," 3," 4" sizes
- Disposable cotton swabs or spirit 10 ml
- Band aid – 6 of various sizes
- Elastic bandage – 1 and a sling
- Savlon antiseptic solution and cream
- Sterilized gauze pads
- A clinical thermometer

- A dropper
- A pair of scissors
- Few safety pins.
- Syrup paracetamol
- Syrup phenargan prescribed by your doctor
- Small size adhesive plaster.

A tweezer (a pair of tongs) to remove thorn, sting or splinter.

How Interaction with Home Environment Determines Smartness and Intelligence | 08

The home atmosphere, if loving and peaceful will stimulate the creativity and learning of developing child. On the other hand violence and scolding can set the mind of the child in reverse direction, making him dull and uninterested. Such atmosphere affects the child throughout his life. Though home atmosphere and child's learning vary greatly depending upon family circumstances but certain basic principles remain the same to create a stimulating environment for the child.

Neglectful parents and hostile atmosphere will decrease the IQ of a child while warm attitude of parents will help improvement in child's IQ. By warm attitude, we mean by loving children explaining smaller things, answering the children's questions and making children to participate in home decisions but not letting the child overpowered or quarrel-some and wild. The suggestions made by children should be heard in family meeting but if these are not accepted, it should be explained to them. The child should know that the family respects his views and he is loved and approved by all. This helps in developing confidence in family and communication as well.

There are many ways that the parents show their children of having congenial atmosphere in the family. It may be by love and helping them in social activities, protection, learning good communication skills, discipline, positive attitude, encouragement, motivation, friendship, development of self esteem and creating human values. These all, have positive affect on personality and IQ development. On the contrary, Physical abuse, neglected family, violence, parental separation and death have bad effects over the child and reduce his IQ. We shall discuss them individually.

There are different ways to show love and care to a child. It may be kissing, cuddling, hugging for a small child but you can always show love in the ways you enjoy better. For bigger children answering their questions, getting them gifts, chocolate, taking them to parks, swings, tolling telling them stories, praising them, giving them treats and playing with them.

A warm and democratic home helps the child to develop as an individual who can evaluate situation and deal with them appropriately. You can always help the child by asking him choice in wearing shoe, cloths or having food. This would help him in taking decisions.

Some parents set their stardoms very high, in order to keep their children striving for them. The youngster gets discouraged feels inadequate and becomes anxious. Try to develop confidence in child's ability so that he become self confident in himself to keep trying for the goal.

Do not use fear of failure, of scolding, of physical punishment, of ridicule, abuse, neglect or showing violence. Parental separation also affects children badly that they become depressed and dull, have excessive crying and tantrum, becoming sad. School children show more of depression, indifference, anger while older children commonly show intense anger and remains unhappy, show behavioural and emotional problems. All such behaviour lower the intelligence.

Anxiety about violence, scolding, ridiculing or physical punishment or any other kind of maltreatment push the children to become violent, depressed, drug addict and show psychiatric problems, reducing their IQ.

8 (a) Making your child street smart

Street proofing (environment proofing) means that your child should protect himself from occurrences outside home. May it be a sexual assault or danger of life. It is important to teach children about such situations. The key words are identifying the situation and reacting to it, which a smart and intelligent child can do. Just teaching to identify a problem is not enough, the child should also learn to react. While walking with your child through neighbourhood, point out the places, people and activities that are usually present at any given time. Assist your child to recognize the normal and abnormal situations. Make your child alert by game observing activities and persons on the street. Spot the problems at isolated places, poorly lit areas, abandoned houses etc.

Always ask the child about his whereabouts. Let the child know his name, address and phone number. Not to use untravelled streets, use only frequently travelled and well lit streets and accompany a family member or a friend. Never allow a stranger to touch you. Cry for help. Do not follow as unknown person. Do not accept anything from unknown person. Try to run and inform the parents.

8 (b) Discipline and behaviour

It is said "there is no love without discipline and there is no discipline without love." Parenting is like a fashion industry where parents should know the normal behaviour pattern of the child and the behaviour which is likely to cause problems and maladjustment in later life, for example thumb sucking is considered normal for 1–2 years old infant but is abnormal after 3–4 years.

Physical and neurological maturation changes create potential for behaviour problems under the influence of hormones. Temperament is of particular importance and refers to child's characteristic style of responding. Most temperamental characteristics show only modest stability over time. An active intense 2 years old does not necessarily grow up into intense 22 years old. An active child may be especially problematic for low key parents. Outgoing parents may pressurize a child who is "slow to warm up." "Goodness of fit" between child and parents may be a powerful prediction of outcome.

To many people, discipline means punishment. But actually, to discipline means to teach. **Rather than punishment, discipline should be a positive way of helping and guiding children to achieve self-control. Discipline does not mean shouting, beating, spanking.**

8 (b) (i) Why children need discipline and good behaviour?

You, as parents, are your child's first teachers. Disciplining you child may be difficult, hence understanding the reasons for its need is important which are as follows:

For protection

Often parents discipline their children to protect them from danger. Parents may teach a young child not to touch the hot stove by removing her from danger while saying "No, stay away. The hot stove will burn you and it will hurt! ".

To get along with others

Discipline can help children learn, to get along with others and develop self-control. A 12 years old reminds her friend, of school rules, that help both to avoid a conflict.

To understand limits

Discipline can help children understand their limits and learn acceptable behaviour. A 6 years old learns to take turns in the class because the teacher and students have set rules for how to behave.

Discipline helps children to

- Think and act in an orderly manner showing acceptable behaviour.
- Understand the logical consequences of their actions.

- Order and use information which is important for their success in school and elsewhere.

- Learn common rules that everyone lives by, such as respect for other's property and to respect elders.

- Learn the values that are held by their family and community.

The purpose of discipline to the children, is to learn an acceptable behavior so that they are able to make wise decisions while dealing with problems.

8 (b) (ii) Discipline is not punishment

Discipline is not the same as punishment. Physical punishment, such as hitting, slapping and verbal abuses are not effective. While such punishment may seem to get fast results, in the long term it is more harmful than helpful. Punishment promotes physical aggression in children by showing them that violence is acceptable way of life and that "might makes right."

Instead of using punishment to correct the behaviour, children need to learn what behaviour is all about and why? Parents should stress "do's" rather than "don'ts." An example of positive discipline would be telling your son, "Please pick your clothes up off the floor because I have to clean the place," rather than saying something negative like, "Don't throw your clothes on the floor any more!".

8 (b) (iii) Parents and school discipline

The discipline that children learn at home is the basis for their behaviour at school. School discipline should be an extension of home discipline.

- Parents should view a discipline problem in school as a home problem too. If your child's teacher reports a discipline problem, such as acting out in the classroom, talk to your child and the teacher and work on a solution together. Try to find comfortable ways of controlling behaviour and redirecting the student's energy towards smart working. This will encourage and develop self-discipline, good work habits and good behaviour.

- Parents should know and support the school's rules. Just as at home, classrooms and schools must have the rules of conduct. Most effective schools are those where students, parents, teachers and administrators help to set the rules. Children are then encouraged to be self-disciplined. Children should know that their parents expect them to follow school rules.

- Parents should know the discipline code, policy or code of conduct of the school. If there is none, parents might suggest that a written behaviour code be developed. This will make rules clear and easily understood.

- Children need clear rules and consistent enforcement to guide their behaviour. In school, as at home, the most effective rules are those decided upon by everyone-students, teachers, administrators and parents – and enforced by all.

8 (b) (iv) Discipline tips for parents

- Set a good example. You are role models for your child. For example, if you want to teach your child that physical violence is not the way to resolve conflicts or problems, then don't use physical punishment.

- Set limits, but be careful not to impose too many rules. Before making a rule, ask yourself: Is it necessary? Does the rule protect a child's health and safety? Does it protect the rights or property of others? Too many rules are hard, if not impossible, to enforce.

- Keep rules simple and understandable.

- Involve the children as much as possible In making family rules. Such rules are less likely to be broken. Help your child to understand the rules and what happens when they are broken? If you and your 4 year old agree that he shouldn't cross the street alone, and he breaks this rule, he should be ready to face the consequences.

- Be flexible. Some rules may work when a child is young but as children get older, they need and want more independence. Remember, not all children respond in the same way.

- **Help your children to develop self-control** – Young children do not have the self-control needed to follow all the rules, all the times. For example a 5 years old may not have the self-control needed, not to take a biscuit from the biscuit jar before dinner. To help the child resist, a parent can move the jar out of sight or offer a snack that is allowed. For an infant, thumb sucking is natural but as he grows older, teach him not to do the same thing because it is abnormal.

- Tell a child about behaviour that is annoying to you.

- Act quickly when a child misbehaves. Don't let a problem build up over time.

- Be consistent. Agree with other family members on methods of discipline. This way a child always knows what will happen if he or she does not follow the rules.

- Let the child know that you appreciate his or her efforts.

- Avoid power struggles with your children. Discipline is not a game in which there is a winner or looser. You expect co-operation from your child and your child expects you to be fair. Respect your child enough to allow disagreements at times.

- Offer positive suggestions. Criticism and nagging can cause your child to become resentful or angry or develop low self-esteem.

- Tell your children how much you love them. When they misbehave, let them know it is their behavior that you dislike, not them.

8 (b) (v) Children learn what they live with

- If a child lives with criticism, he learns to condemn.

- If a child lives with hostility, he learns to fight.

- If a child lives with ridicule, he learns to be shy.

- If a child lives with shame, he learns to feel guilty.

- If a child lives with encouragement, he learns confidence.

- If a child lives with tolerance, he learns to be patient.

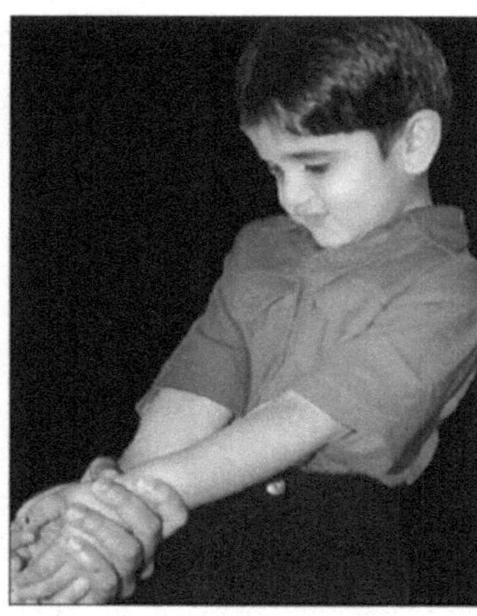

No hostility please

- If a child lives with praise, he learns to appreciate.
- If a child lives with fairness, he learns justice.
- If a child lives with security, he learns to have faith.
- If a child lives with approval, he learns to like himself.
- If a child lives with acceptance and friendship, he learns to find love in the world.

8 (c) Leadership and encouragement

To create a successful personality, leadership qualities should be cultivated fromchildhood by giving right exposure, encouragement and opportunity to a child.

How do you provide all this to your child?

- Focus on the child's assets rather than on short comings.
- Do not unduly criticize the child, that hampers development. his confidence aid trust.
- Let the child explore new places, meet new people and have first hand experiences.
- Give the child freedom to take decisions under your guidance/ supervision.
- Designate tasks to the child, inculcating responsibility and enhancing capability.
- Encourage the child's curiosity
- A questioning mind brings growth and innovation

8 (d) Self-esteem in a child

All children develop at their own rate and ability and every child has own approach to life. This basically means development of various skills in a child which make the foundation of positive self-image so that he could progress and become achiever in life. Self-esteem is to be imbibed at an early stages of life, since the same habits ate carried to later life of an individual. The skills which need attention are:

Self Esteem

8 (d) (i) Communication

Self Esteem It is a key to success. In a small child, the body language may communicate the love, mood or thoughts. Around 15 months of age, jargon speech, which is child's own language, develops. By next 4–5 months he can utter few (10–15) words which are desirable/undesirable and by age of two years some children can speak 80–100 words and by the age 3–4 years some children can communicate easily. At this stage the phonics of the child should be corrected by repeatedly correcting the faulty words. **The child should be encouraged to speak correctly and fluently. In children, habit of loud reading, if inculcated, can help them to speak fearlessly and fluently. School going child should be encouraged to take part in debates and group discussions. Thus they will develop communication skills.** Language is important part of this skill. The medium can be English, Hindi or any regional language. Recalling and summarization need practice.

8 (d) (ii) Conflict resolution

Since the liking of children can be different as compared to adults, they may not like certain things at home, school or in society. This results in anxiety, anger or depression and difficulty in concentrating and lot of time is wasted in these conflicts, hence their resolution is important. The conflicts may be internal or external.

If the child is taught to express his feelings, he will be better adjusted in society and can make a better human being. This will largely avoid behaviour problems. If there is love and acceptance for the child and also respect for him as an individual, he will be able to solve his conflicts which will open the ways of his progress and self-esteem. Parents need to develop real understanding of their children in order to help them solve their problems. Children do learn to cope up certain situations in society and school.

Interaction with peers without close adult supervision calls on increasing quarreling skills. A balance between fantasy and appropriate ability to negotiate real world indicate healthy emotional development. The best way to ease conflicts is to communicate with parents, teachers and peers. SWOT' analysis for conflict resolution refers to Strength, Weakness, Opportunities and Threats. The resolution should be made thinking above points in a particular conflict. The child should have strength to tell the right thing in congenial atmosphere. He should know his weaknesses and that of others also. He should always be responsible and should have power to identify himself as a person.

8 (d) (iii) Academics

Academic forms an important part of esteem building in a child. School is the place where child learns academics, rules, good behaviour, adjustment to life problems and character building. The child comes in contact with different believes, values and religions. **He starts understanding the values of society along with academics. He also understands his position in carrier choosing and what he wants to be in his later life to contribute to society as "respectable person."**

8 (d) (iv) Physical achievements

Gradually child learns to keep himself fit mentally and physically. "A sound body has a sound mind" is well known saying. Hence importance of play and games is well understood towards body, mind and skill development. This is of value to prepare a child in more challenging activities and esteem building in life.

Physical fitness is important in acquiring skills. A child around 3–4 years of age may co-operate with other children and enjoy the games. Older children as they learn the rules and co-operation, come to understand significance of team work as marker in esteem building. Obese children (over-weight) have physical, social and emotional health problems which effect adversely their childhood and self-esteem. Parents must insist on children to play outdoor games and must find time to sit with them. Older children should choose the games they prefer and should play with their counterparts.

8 (d) (v) Self-image and self confidence

What matters most is how do you see yourself. It is the central ingredient of self-esteem and may be won through possessions, personal attractiveness, accomplishments and some social skills. Compliance is always rewarded. Some children conform readily and enjoy easy social success and those who adopt individualistic styles or have visible differences, are stigmatized as "peculiar." They may be puzzled by lack of popularity, meet failures and conferred by their fellows as "funny," stupid or bad. This may become incorporated into child's self-image. Initial discipline, good behaviour, love, care and acceptance by family and peers largely help the child to build positive self-image. Participation in theatre, gymnastics, music, acting, dancing, drama, crafts and other positive creative activities also help in building self image.

8 (d) (vi) Motivation

Motivation in children is very important which make them more successful. The success in life makes them more motivated and inculcates self-esteem in them. Few children are uncooperative and feel no responsibilities of the house or family and it is difficult to get any work from them which culminates in a struggle. Even several requests do not move them. Such children are un-motivated.

On the other side, few children feel responsible about the family, house, studies and their daily activities. Such children are achievers and are motivated because they understand what is wrong and what is right for them and their family. For example, if the child is obese (fatty child), he thinks about his obesity that it causes complications in life such as hypertension and diabetes mellitus or heart problems, this is an internal thought i. e., internal motivation. But if that obese child loses while running with others and feels that he has lost due to his overweight. This is an external stimulus or external motivation.

So there are two types of motivations, Internal and External. In other words we call them as stimuli with which the child decides, the wrong and the right. Both types of motivations are required for the child's progress.

Help the child in following ways:

1. Appreciate the work of the child. This will make him successful which will boost internal motivation and hence hard work.

2. Divide the task into series of small steps. Think of getting work done and not perfection. For example, getting ready for school next day means – setting the bag at night, polishing the shoes and next morning toilet, bath, teeth brushing, clothing and break-fast. It takes few days to become in some order.

3. Incentives be given in the form of praise, toys and privileges. Make an agreement with the child on day-to-day or weekly basis for good work.

4. Know the child's interests and make him to learn those activities.

8 (d) (vii) Social adaptability

The relationship with family peers and society are predominately external at age around two years. By the age of 5 year these controls become internalized. Success to achieve this goal lies in prior emotional development i. e. ability to use internalized images of trusted adult to provide security at the time of stress.

Excessive tight limits can undermine child's sense of initiative whereas loose limits can provocate anxiety and the child feels that there is no one to control. Control is a central issue. Fear, overtiredness or physical discomfort evolve tantrum. The swirl of these emotions is beyond child's ability to analyse or express results in labile mood. Adolescents often socialize in same sex peer groups. Belonging is all important, sharing of confidence and love helps the child to grow fairly.

8 (e) Friendship

Friendship is not about personal gains or status or a superficial interaction. It is a relationship built upon genuine sincerity of the persons involved. If a child has just one good friend, his happiness is two folds. Friendship doubles happiness and reduces sadness. Schooling might become fun if children have friends there and further more they develop spirit of competition when they see their friends studying. It gives them pressure to exceed them. The bonds of friendship between students is often strong enough to surmount the various tragedies. When things are at their worst, schoolmate friends are the greatest source of encouragement and they depend upon each other. Friendship is most powerful and most valuable treasure in life, without which a child becomes unbalanced and self-centered.

Friendship and Co-operation

The friendship made in one's school days is generally free from artifice. The friends could talk to each other on anything which they are unable to discuss with parents or brother and sisters and thus open a channel of communication. In friendship, one has to be sincere and honest otherwise rejection and disappointment becomes inevitable.

The child learns many things such as social behaviour, co-operation, love, playing, conflict resolution and communication skills, from his friends. The friends encourage each other to reach common goals. The relationship with other children, brother, sister, mother, father or relatives may also be like friends but the true friendship implies a relationship which empathies with friends in suffering and encourage them not to lose heart. The friendship determines the way by which one lives his life and this needs to be developed and be infused to grow with it.

Parents Are Child's First and Best Teachers   **09**

The knowledge about intelligence development is gathering fast by studying biology of the brain. **It has shown that brain stimulation has an important role in intelligence development before he reaches eight years of age. The parents are most helpful in child's learning and helping him for rest of his life. It was previously thought that intelligence is fixed for life but it is not so,** we agree that genetically good biological brains are easy to stimulate but if left alone will get slow. If the child is given ample opportunities during these early years, his growth is almost assured.

The child spends most if his day in the family with the parents, hence parents have unique opportunity to mold the child's intelligence and they are the first and the best teachers for the child who will develop at his acceleration, rate of growth. If they use early teaching techniques to their preschool children, they will be satisfied with the child progress later on. Educators are continuously finding the ways and means to raise child intelligence and making them smart. The ways may be physiologic, biologic, early education but it should be understood that the child should start learning at early as possible. We should make them more enthusiastic and happier about learning. The methods should be based on receptive minds and should not undermined the child's ability to learn.

It is not the questions of making a 3 years child as status symbol to complete with neighbours's from 4 years old child. Early learning simply means to stimulate your young child's drive to explore, to sensitize him to learn, to understand the facts and experiences for the brain as food for thoughts, as we require nutritious food for body to keep it healthy and fit. We hope that you will not too much stuff his brain more than he requires, in a similar way the body gets obese if too much food is consumed. **The stimulation of brain should sensitize his learning to stimulate brain growth.**

Early learning means that what really is required for that particular age should be given to the child to raise his intelligence and develop his personality to make him smarter. So that the child remain happier in his life. We shall deal with appropriate stimulation of children of different ages in forth coming text,

i. e. stimulation after birth to six months of age, six months to one year, one year to 18 months, 18 months to three years and three years to six years.

Some parents leave their children alone crying in playpen or room to teach them to be become good and less demanding, by this they are restricting their mental development. The baby always required some activity until he is tired or goes to sleep. These activities may be sounds, movements, play, to touch, to hold, by which he gets some kind of experience to satisfy his insatiable derive to explore. Curtailing such activities of a small child hampers his rate of development and final levels of his smartness and intelligence.

We know of many intelligent and well educated parents who have probably handicapped their children because of poor rearing practices such as neglecting the children by remaining busy from morning to night and going to clubs at late night and coming back home in the morning, leaving their children on themselves or with the hostile servants. Such parent then expect their children to come up to their expectation. The children are scolded which further complicate the problems. Such parents, do not have the time to sit with their children. We are giving an example of one of our rich friend couple, both of them were lawyers and were busy in the morning with their courts and at night with the club, when they reached home, their children were sleeping. The time when children were leaving for school, the parents were sleeping. **They hardly could see each other. Their children were depressed and dejected. They were very slow in playing, talking and studying for which they were scolded and the matter was worsening day by day. The children developed anxiety and lost their self-confidence.**

Such parents are not aware of the child care practices. But there are few parents who over stimulate the children, by pushing them hard to learn even if the children are not ready for it. Such children also meet the same anxiety and loose their confidence because they do not find the right atmosphere of brain growth.

It has been shown by researches that child's ability to acquire skills depends upon opportunities in his own environment and inner schedule of development. **The young child will participate only if he wishes to do so. The parents must use such moments, as children of three or four years eagerly teach themselves and learn during that time, for which joy, enthusiasm and happiness are the requisites. Early learning does not have any ill effect on general health, emotions of the child.**

The parents of higher socioeconomic group felt that to teach a child is the duty of the teacher and not of parents which is not right. **Parents who happily and enthusiastically welcome the child's questions and answer them politely to the satisfaction of the child are always the gainers and so are the children.** Small children love to learn and keep an insatiable desire to learn unless parents discourage, spank or shout at them.

The parents should be careful in finding out what interests your child, which is often about something they want to know or to learn, for which they work hard even to forget their feeds. A five-six months old baby will try his best to overturn again and again as he/she wants to master the skill even if parents put them right because he wants to learn of his own. A child wants to walk if he is made to stand by holding a chair or any other object whatever you do to stop him. He is likely to fall initially but he will stand again to walk and to master his skill.

A baby practices his speech noises repeatedly until he comes out with a word, for which parents also try to help him. No one forces him to practice, the babies try the words endlessly.

The children try to explore the world around them and want to know about them for which they ask question upon question and if they get answer they feel satisfied. A three to four years old child calls for play at his own initiative as he pretends to be grown up. **He will imitate adult at work, try to wash clothes, try to clean the house, oras doctor, as pilot and as teacher and so on. Watching the child, the parents can find out as to what holds child concentration for long time. This is the activity where he wants to develop his skill with curiosity and wants to show his parents for his achievement.**

Often parent teach their children only to go to school on time, taking breakfast in the morning, to keep still while sitting but do their school home work themselves hurriedly. They hardly give any brain stimulation. **Numerous researches have shown that five-six years old children who are deprived by stimulation have learning difficulties and limp academically throughout school or drop out and unable to adjust themselves in the jobs later on. But if such children are stimulated by their parents starting from first year onwards. They do very well later on in life.**

As parents you are the best teachers of your children who can do wonders in child's life to keep them happy and contented. Unless the children are mentally stimulated during preschool years, further school learning may be half hearted by the child. Early intellectual development of child takes place at home. **This means that if parents spend their considerable quality time with the child, they can help the child in mental development. But those parents who are economically burdened or are too busy in their business or leisure and do not devote time for their children stimulation, are pushing their children towards some kind of backwardness.**

Stimulating the child also means good care, loving, eating together, solving problem of children, playing with them, answering their questions which culturally deprived children do not get. The child learns by his senses such as touch, small, taste, vision and learning. The child wants to master the thing with all of these senses which is essential for perceptional growth and wide range of experience and perception, he gets with parents when he is with them. Perceptional development is essential for school success also during early years, and there is often a vast difference of perceptional development in culturally deprived children and those who were fortunate enough to get opportunity to explore with their special senses.

9 (a) Communication

After exploring, the child wants to share his experiment with the close persons such as parents, brother or sister but he cannot explain to them due to non development of proper language. **So language development and communication is another area where parents need to stimulate the child.** The parents who neglect their children, always hold them back in speech. Careful parents always stimulate the child for speech and communication, they cheer the child, repeat the words till he is able to speak the correct word. That means a stimulated child always gets a feedback which corrects him and stimulates him for speech while this is not so with culturally deprived children. The child communicates depending upon his age.

Communication is the key to success which makes child smart and intelligent. To communicate with baby, you have to watch and learn from his tones, body language and levels of stress. Your baby is always communicating with you, if you notice little things. The communication can be through

1.   Body language

2.   Crying

3.   Speech

Body Language

The body language can communicate love, bad mood or thoughts.

Communication

i) Communication of love

Babies do not know how to hide their emotions while most of the parents do not know how to show their emotions. The more you convey your love to the baby, the more happily he responds. **Hugs are the best to show the love even if the child is crying.** Your child tries to reach you and communicate without knowing how to talk. When you see your baby dancing his feet, you know that he is happy.

Parents who make a habit of communicating their love to each member of the family, their life becomes much smoother. If you try to have fun and establish love or jokes with your child, he may also smile or wink or raise his eye brows or make certain noises as communication like to be bounced gently, not shaken or patted too hard.

(ii) Communication of bad mood

The babies tend to get cranky by over stimulation. It is possible that the child needs to sleep. Some-times little pacification, such as smiling or waving may help them. Few babies are just "always cranky." This shows frustration and requires pacification, such babies get better as they grow and learn to speak.

(iii) Communication of thoughts

If your baby just looks at you without expression, when you are trying to get him smile, he is probably concentrating on bowel movement. If the baby leans towards you with open mouth, he is probably hungry or he is trying to kiss you. Some time a child brings your shoes to you that means he wants to go out and if he points towards something which means he wants to acquire that. If your baby rubs his eyes and moves his head back or forth, probably he wants no activity and wants to sleep.

Communication through crying

When the baby is born, the first cry he makes, is the most important. This shows that he is breathing well. Crying sometimes is actually good for babies because it helps develop their lungs. Do not try to run to rescue every time your baby cries, let him try to work out his problem for himself.

The child cries when he is either wet, hungry, sick or has nose block or pain somewhere. Baby soothers should be avoided as far as possible because these can lead to diarrhoea, vomiting and malaligned teeth.

9 (b) Speech – development and delay

Though the child starts referring mama, dada from 40 weeks (10 months) onwards, but jargon and some familiar words are spoken at 15 months of age. The vocabulary at 18 months of age is 10–15 words and it swells to more than 100 words by two years of age. Some children at the age of 3–4 years can participate verbally as well as physically in an activity. Children can and will respond to seriously posed questions. By about age of 13 years, the child is primary informant and should be dealt with directly.

As the child grows, parents should look for all opportunities to help him to learn. Children vocabulary is as broad as you make it. Encourage them to speak. Parents should be quiet when the baby is trying to speak. Use of polite words like "please" "excuse me," "thanks" "good morning" "welcome" should be taught to them. Babies who are introduced to other or foreign language can actually learn it in much easier way. Children learn to speak lies much later. **Regular interaction of the child with picture books help to provide an ideal material for language development. Parents should facilitate child's language development by speaking clear, simple sentences, asking questions and responding positively to the child's incomplete sentences.** Normal hearing children usually develop language by two to three years of age. Children with delayed language acquisition often have greater psychological and behavioural problems. Deafness, chromosomal abnormality, meningitis, brain haemorrhage, low birth weight, lead intoxication and environmental deprivation are common causes of delayed speech development. Child's vocabulary grows in verbal rich environment.

Gradually the child learns to put his emotions and intentions into language and uses words as tool of thought. But a culturally deprived child is likely to answer with single word or ignore it, because he has not been stimulated to think and talk about his experiences.

Many parents make efforts to motivate the child and stimulate his learning, for which they get rapid response. Learning involves the developing of child's ability to engage in purposeful action. It is the home in which parents and family members provide the basic learning otherwise the child is likely to be handicapped in later learning and educational development. Learning always ignites the mind which is a powerful resource. The parents play the role of teachers in child's learning.

Varun, six months old is made to lie down often in a crib or playpen. He just sucks his finger and looks into space or cries. Arjun two years old is always denied by parents, 'no - no' it will break, was asked by the parents. The child gets no chance to explore. Fatima four years is coercively stimulated and is forced constantly with activities. They all are deprived of normal stimulation. Ravina five years stimulated with love and care and is answered for everything she asks. She is taken to various places outdoors. She plays and mixes with parents. She behaves in a nice way and is good at learning everything at home and in her school also. But other children who all are deprived of stimulation have problems of learning and behaviour. **This shows, how right stimulation by parents can make child happy and good at learning.**

Overstimulation is as had as understimulation. When normal stimulation with love and care for whole period of childhood is given in easy way, it can raise the level of intelligence potential to the tune of bright or gifted child regardless of his innate potential. Large number of potentially superior and average children lose due to lack of sufficient early stimulation. **Making home atmosphere culturally rich with wholesome environment in early years with early teaching ways can do much to raise smartness and intelligence**

in children which can only be possible with loving parents. Even a good nursery school is too little to give. Fathers and mothers who have tried using early learning principles are always delighted with the progress of the child, their happy relationship and enjoy them more. They need not to push or pressurized or hurt the child in anyway to teach him.

Learning and Role of Parents 10

Ignited mind is powerful resource

One of the challenges for new parents is learning and teaching the child to relax instead of getting frustrated. The child is born as gift of nature and we are all individuals and thus we must respect the individuality of the child.

To have a contented baby, you learn his personality and provide him with toys or books that support his natural qualities. If you have a busy child, give him toys, bells and whistles. If your child is quiet type, give him lots of books, mirror and things to paint. If the child is cranky, give him less stimulation. Try to put the child in some schedules. There are two schedules of learning. The first is the baby's natural schedule like feeds, passage of urine and stool and the other is the family's real life schedule. The other schedule i. e. family schedule, in which child learns new family habits and loses his bad habits. Your job as parent is to get him both work simultaneously. From the very first day, child keeps his own schedule such as feeding or bowel movements. Watch for both the schedules and help the child to keep them up. The child will be more contented this way.

(a) Changing the routine

For real life schedules you have to try to break his bad habits. Such changes are made when you are in new surroundings. For example if the child's is addicted to bottle or a pacifier, in that case you can "lose" a bottle or a pacifier while you are on vacations at some new place. In new surroundings, the baby may be preoccupied and may forget those items easily and may stop demanding them altogether.

(b) Parents as teacher, – do's and dont's

1. If you are anxious parents, you will probably have an anxious baby. Take ten deep breaths and smile at your baby every time you look at him.

2. If your newborn child is not used to swing, do not give up, try again and again. Babies change everyday.

3. Babies get bored quickly so keep on changing the activities.

4. Do not underestimate your child, if your baby has accompanied you on some road for few times, he remembers the way and probably could teach you.

5. Do not call your child bad kid or tell him bad, because he believes and hears everything you say.

6. Let your child be challenged. That's how he learns.

7. Babies learn from their own mistakes faster than parents do.

8. Teach your child to follow directions early, such as cleaning up and schooling.

9. Teach your child to be positive, not negative.

10. Traditions are important kind of routines, build up traditions with your child.

11. Help your child to rely on himself.

12. The child does not really hate anything. Initially he is just frightened because he is unsure of it. Teach your baby to enjoy him so that he gets accustomed.

13. Do not hold your baby too much, else he will never learn to be alone, which may make school going difficult.

Set examples

- Babies watch and imitate everyone around them.

- Everything you say is being registered. Your words, thoughts and expression will be replayed for you at a later date.

- Your baby watches you every day. He wants to be just like you and tries to repeat the same activities like you do. Remember, babies grab everything you have because they imitate you.

- Do not get surprised if you discover your own faults in your child. This is something like looking in a mirror.

- Try not to argue with anyone, especially your spouse, in front of your child. This upsets him. Teach your child to love and respect the mother, father, elders and youngers.

- Let the child witness the creative people doing productive things. You are your baby's example.

- Take your child to worship places. This will inculcate in him to be respectful and to be quiet.

- Make your baby independent. Show him how to hold the bottle so that he is able to drink from it.

- Applaud every time if your baby is doing something, looks at you and smiles. He feels that he has accomplished something.

- Try to encourage your baby to move, by placing some of his favourite toys at some distance slightly out of reach.

- Try to set examples for the child and do not compare his behaviour or habits with other children in a negative way. Every child has own potentials of development.

- Do not allow your child to dictate direct on to others. After all he is no expert.

- If there are more children in the family, try to give equal love and responsibilities to all and there should be no disparity in behaviour.

- Try not to be over protective, but keep an eye over the child all times to avoid accident. Let your child explore under your watchful eyes.

- If your child slips and falls, help him immediately but calmly. Make him feel as if he has helped himself. Thus your child will develop self-confidence and sense of security.

(c) Concentration development

Some children have small span of concentration. They cannot sit for long at one place and are not able to concentrate on one particular subject for long time. The concentration of the child can be enhanced which is very important for making him successful. The following ways will help the child to develop concentration.

1. Make sure that the child is not sick and anxious, also he had comfortable sleep and is eating well.

2. **Motivate the child by praising him, with which he feels successful and works harder and concentrates at his work.**

3. Divide the work into small steps.

4. Do not count on failures but encourage him to do his job.

5. Incentive in the form of his liking such as toys or privileges on weekly or daily basis will help the child to work harder and develop concentration.

6. Make teaching interesting by examples, pictures or showing places and other activities.

7. Teach the child to pray and take him to places of worship.

8. **Key to develop concentration is praise and encouragement.**

9. Make home atmosphere congenial.

Outdoor activities

Let your child explore out doors and nature and see birds, butterflies, frogs, dogs or cats. Let him notice wind, trees and their shaking branches. Make him see ocean and touch the sand. Let him enjoy green grass.

Outdoor Activity

- Let your child get dirty, give him plenty of clothes to play.

- Let your child see aquarium and swimming fish.

- Teach your baby swimming.

- Teach your child photography.

- Show your child from the window, children going to school or persons walking or going on buses.

Indoor activities

The children also learn from family members. The child should spend time with parents and grand parents. In this way he will learn values of life by listening to them and by watching. This is all important for their mental and social growth. Show your baby running water in: he bathroom and let him listen to the sound of it.

(i) Radio, T. V. and computers

Children also learn from Radio, TV programmes and computers. Parents should make them interact with the programmes of their choice. Older children can learn from Internet also. Computer games are quite popular among the children.

(ii) Pets

Many children love to play with pets and gain lot of information. Care of pets will stimulate love and affection in them. Take them to zoo to show various animals.

(iii) Reading and story telling

- **Some children want to hold the books and look at pictures because they see their parents reading. Encourage them for reading, choose a specific time for reading every day.**

- Use even a grocery store as a learning tool. Ask the child to read various names and tell him about the things you purchased. Show them exhibition, museum and historical places.

- Youngsters love to hear stories. It does not matter what story is all about.

(iv) Plantation

- Elder children should be encouraged to take interest in nature such as plantation. Plant growth, watering, plant multiplication, flowering and to enjoy the beauty.

(v) Music

- Music helps in calming the children.

- Babies love to sing. Try them singing.

- If you sing to him, the child would learn about it. While singing, use body language as well. Put some music and watch your child getting into the rhythm.

(vi) Toys and games

- Use toys as learning tools (refer chapter 11-12 Toys and Games)
- In indoor games - Table tennis, Ludo, Ball, Cards, Badminton, carom board, chess and business games, etc.

In outdoor games – Foot ball, Tennis, Hockey, Badminton, Cricket etc.

(d) Toilet training

The child should be trained for passing stool and urine in the toilet, otherwise he is likely to soil his clothes quite often. The control is usually achieved between 2 to 3 years of age. For passage of stools, the child should be made to sit comfortably on specially available baby seats for about 10 to 15 minutes. During this time mother should be by the side of the child engaging him/her with some activity. The child should be praised after passage of stool or urine.

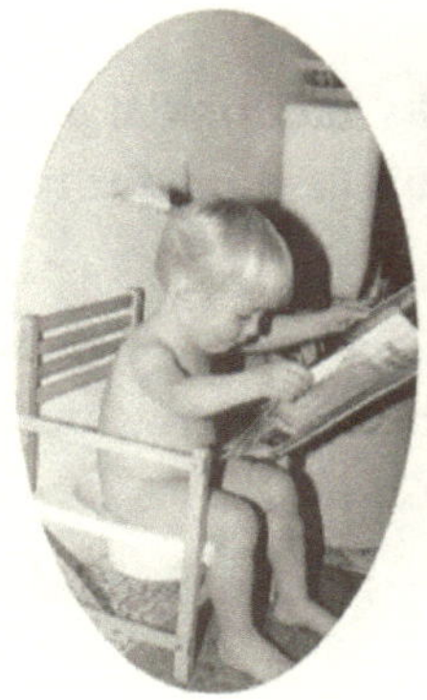

Toilet Training Seat

Two types of toilet seats are available. One is attachment to the adult toilet seat, the other is low seat. The later one is better since the child can sit by himself keeping his feet on the floor. For urination, the very small child should be held in squatting position in such a way that the back of the child is held against the abdomen of the mother and is made to pass urine or the child be trained" on the toilet seat. The procedure is repeated every 2 to 3 hours or as desired. The child becomes conditioned to such procedure after sometimes. Though bowel and bladder control comes simultaneously in the third year, the bladder control is slightly slower than, that of bowel. Occasional child can become dry by night around twelve months. By fifteen to eighteen months many children would retain urine for couple of hours and become dry by nights in third year.

Stimulating Intellectual Growth Birth to Eighteen Months | 11

After birth a newborn requires feeding, bath, love, sleep, diaper, changing and protection, which all parents try to do in their best possible way but baby's fast growing brain is not taken care of which is not so obvious. Baby's early environment and sensory stimulus can cause physical changes in his brain, growing his mental capacity. The baby's brain will grow three times in few years. As already mentioned in the text that baby's brain may be compared with computer, it has to be programmed. The more inputs are given to it, more information is the output.

Sensory experience is always necessary for perception and making of concepts. You should remember that baby is living and growing child who needs activity, stimulation and experience. **The child learns by gathering sensory stimuli, perception, curiosity of exploration of new objects, formation of concepts, association of words and freedom of learning. More the sensory stimulation, better are the perceptions, more the perception, better and more are the concepts. Once the concept are formed, the future functions start.**

According to Dr. Dunn, the brain in early life can record experiences in a better way and parents should give all possible sensory stimuli, opportunities and experience to child in early stage of life which he will experience by touching, hearing, seeing, tasting and smelling senses.

The usual practice in our families is that we put the newborn baby in a crib where he is unable to react with surroundings or he is put in a cot or a pram, he is cut of from the surroundings. We always feel that he should be fully secured without bothering about his sensory stimuli but when he is able to sit then also he is restricted to playpen or a seat but he is some-what better in reacting with surrounding, though we all have the feeling that the baby should grow and he will grow at his own time. **It is alright when he is sleeping, that he should not be disturbed but when he is awake he should be given sensory stimuli because a small child can visualize the vague shadows and shapes within a weeks of birth and with these stimuli, the brain of the child will grow.**

For this, many researches have been made and it has been found that babies pay more attention to bright and moving objects and they enjoy these visuals. They can distinguish between smells, tones and by their touch they even can distinguish between round nipples for milk and a rubber catheter. The children recognises mother's hands and becomes quiet if he is crying. This is all due to learning process going in the few week's infant.

Studies have even been made that as to how much the child grows automatically and how much difference it makes to enrich his environment up to six months of age. Few babies, in awaiting adoption were exposed to both types of environment who were physically and mentally normal. The control group was confined to cot laying on their backs, changed when required, were fed four hourly and bathed routinely. The infants started paying attention to surroundings in other few weeks and started discovering their hands. The waking time also increased and they started watching their fingers – in thirteen to fifteen weeks of age. They could follow the close moving object up to certain degrees by one month. By four months their visual accommodation was comparable to normal. They could raise their hands by eleven weeks of age and could turn their head to see an object. They tried to grasp a moving object by 21 weeks of age.

In another group the infants were given stimulated environment such as removal from cot and putting them on stomach for sometime to facilitate them to watch the surroundings, they were exposed to rattles for grasping, toys, few sounds and noises and colours. The infant appeared to be more attentive and active as compared to control group and could grasp the object at fourteen weeks of age is i. e. about two month earlier than control group. The fast gain by these infants was due to stimulated environment matching to basic needs of the infant. **The experiment shows that the even a small infant can grow fast if given enriched environment.**

If you watch your infant carefully giving him enough stimuli for learning, he would grow faster but the best guide is to see the baby's reactions.

(A) How to stimulate your child from birth to six months

There are many ways to give sensory as well as motor stimulation to your child. Find out when the baby is interested in the surroundings. He is neither sleepy nor hungry. This time is usually before feed or after feed, burped and changed. During first few days you can pick him up, can put to your shoulder or in lap, he may look around for short time which shall give him a sensory stimulus. Hang some bright colourful toys over his bed which could move to and fro. Hang some bright and coloured pictures on the wall. Change the position of cot to give the child different view of the room. Let him kick and play sometimes.

As he is able to hold his head you can hold him in your arms and shoulder or in a canvas sling at your back and carry him around the house. This would give him lots of sensory stimuli occasionally. You can carry him into inclined pram with seat belt to give him wider view.

Language development takes place as you talk to your baby for registering words in his brain which also takes place in early weeks of life. Put some loving words in his ears when you are feeding, changing or cuddling, and embracing. Try to establish communication with your child often as possible.

Soon, the child starts cooing and babbling sounds which are the basic of language development. You should talk to him so that he gets the idea of what the language is. You can sing to your baby and play music for him/her.

Milestones

Age of months	Gross Motor	Fine Motor	Language & Communication	Perception
2 months	Head hold improving		Smile response	Stares near by face
3 months	No head lag	Reaches for object and misses	Says 'aah nhag'	
4 months	No head lag	Reaches for objects, hands in midline	Laughs aloud	Stares at own hand
6 months	Sits with support	Transfers object from one hand to another	Single word babble	Take every thing to mouth

Millstones at age of birth to six months

Physical movements, touch sensations, visual and hearing stimuli are stored in the baby's brain and get organized, by which the baby learns to perceive the various things. As the child grows, he needs more of such stimuli to acquire the knowledge. So, for building up such information, the child needs great freedom and opportunities to touch, to manipulate, to grasp, to release, to search, to reach, keeping in view of his safety and health.

The children who are not given such opportunities are likely to be delayed in their activities and thoughts. The child may be put on padded flat surfaces, padded floor where he can move his arms and kick freely. Certain families tie their young ones with cloth restraining their upper and lower limbs thinking that child may not get afraid, which is not desired. Such families prevent the child from basic stimulations. You can put the child on stomach and eventually he will learn to roll over. Give him some soft rubber or wooden toy, foam rubber, cloth, tissue paper for grasping, to give him stimulus for texture. Since the small child puts everything in the mouth, hence avoid painted, pointed or objects smaller than his fist to avoid its swallowing.

During fifth or sixth months, the child increases his activity of legs and hands and other activities. Encourage him reach for objects. These are basic motivation for the child's learning as he wants to see, hear and move. From birth to six months following toys are recommended.

Since at 2–3 months, the sound, smell and feel of the mother sometime appears promptly in response to crying. This time, intensity of smiling, eyes widening and lips puckering show rise and fall together. Every few seconds, as the excitement builds up, the infant turns, settles and interacts. A month later he can hold a rattle and can shake it. Babies watch bright moving objects and listens to musical sound. The toy should be colourful, soft, washable, easy to handle and should make some noise.

Suggested toys are rattles, rings, plastic keys, plastic toys for suspending on pram or cot, rubber, washable toys like balls, animals figures and sound making toys.

(B) Stimulation at 6–12 months of age

Milestones

Age of months	Gross motor	Fine motor	Language & communication	Perception
7 months	Rolls over and creeps	Grasps large objects	Multiple words sounds	Prefers mother, enjoys mirror
9 months	Sitting without support	Thumb – finger grasp, pokes objects		Bangs two cubes, Holds bottle or cup
10 months	Sits up alone, crawls	Picks up pellet	Mama – dada	Ask, for distant object, Peekaboo games
12 months	Walks with one hand held	Pincer movements, drops toys	Two words Mama, Dada	Simple games

Around nine months the child can sit without support and his area of vision also increases. He shall be fascinated by looking and handling various objects and shall record sensory stimuli in his brain. He will pick up the objects and drop them down again and again. By this he relates finger movement and bang on the floor. At this stage the child may be given variety of things, toys to touch, throw, grasp, shake, to listen, to smell, to see various colours.

Toys at 6–12 months of age

The child puts every things in the mouth, wants to inspect, pass the object from one hand to other, bangs and drops, shows toys or objects to parents, crumbles papers and watches picture book with the help of parents. He also enjoys musical instruments like drums.

Recommended toys for this age group are:

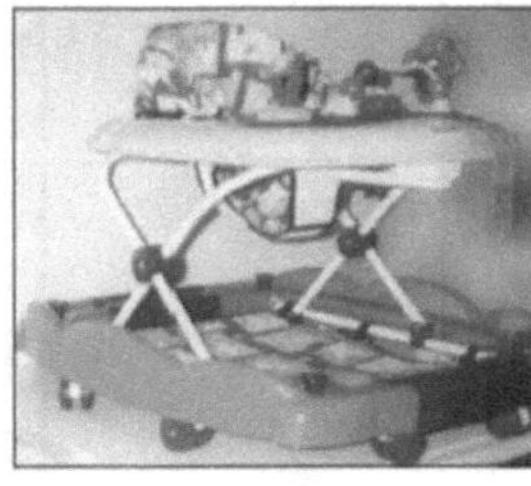 

- Balls
- Dolls
- Ring sets
- Picture books
- Push and pull toys – toy car, wheeled toys
- Flashlight making toys, stuffed toys
- Sound making toys – rattle, drums, whistle, sound making animals and birds – figures
- Rocking toys – for balancing
- Pots, Pans, spoons, mirror, cardboard box and plastic containers.

The child may find much amusement with just a cardboard or a paper box or pot and spoon that he may forget about expensive toys. Parents need not to spend much for the costly toys.

As soon as the child starts crawling, he should be cheered to move forward by putting some things nearby for his picking. This will be a sensory and well as a motor activity. During waking hours he should spend on such activities. He shall thus develop coordination of movements. Do not try to hurry to put him into the baby walker. **Crawling is important for coordination and brain stimulation. He should be provided with a big space as possible with**

controlled temperature, cleanliness and lot of toys. It may be carpeted or wooden or simply cemented. Make the crawling safe by removing the objects he may break or swallow or injure himself. Electric points be covered and stair doors closed. Remove phone and electrical chords also. Do not discourage him by saying no – no too often. **If you snatch objects out of his hands, scold or slap him then he will carry the idea of that curiosity and being investigator is wrong which will frustrate him in his attempt to learn.** The parents should use grassy lawn also for crawling of the child. Remember since the child put, everything in the mouth, he may put mud, medicines, cleaning agents, polish and other household items which should be removed. **Crawling is important for the baby to get sensory stimulation.**

During sleeping hours the child can be put in playpen or cot but when he gets up and cries he should be pacified by giving him toys.

By using all his senses he shall now anticipate the sound of steps and make difference in the sounds of mother and father, touching knobs, holding table and chair legs, he shall make all such activities. He may have likes and dislikes. He may cry when parents leave for the job. For his speech development, parents should encourage him by talking to him in simple words like bottle, nipple, cup, water, mama, daddy etc. The words will be registered in his brain and shall develop his speech later on. By this, the child develops the idea that things do have their names. The more you talk to him, earlier he would develop his speech. Children books at this stage may be very useful. Picture books encourage the child when he can see common things. You can read for him so that he could associate reading means knowledge about the things and it should be made pleasurable. At this stage he tries to develop many skills of pushing, pocking, pulling which he tries to do with concentration. This will develop his finger. He would even like to break the toys to get some idea about throwing. He is doing all that for learning. The most curious and eager he is about his surrounding exploration, more he is accumulating the knowledge in his brain, the more intelligent he will develop into

(C) Stimulation at one year to eighteen months

The child grows rapidly during first eighteen months and are most important for measuring his intellectual abilities. At about one year, the child starts pulling up to standing and tries to make staggering steps holding chair, table and finally starts walking with skill. His milestones at fifteen to eighteen months will be as follows.

15 months	Walks alone, crawls upstairs	Hugs parents	Jargon speech	Make tower of 3 cubes
18 months	Uses stairs with one hand held, Run stiffly, explores drawer.	Feeding self, complains when soiled	10 words speech, Identifies one or more body parts	Makes tower of 3 or 4 cubes

Milestones from 15 months to 18 months

At this age he tries to explore everything he can approach and his curiosity is insatiable. He can grasp, climb, pick, pull, push even the small objects. His span is short. Some parents keep such children in playpen and let them cry, they feel that children should be taught the way they should live. Such a displeasure and the unstimulating stimuli leave psychological affect on the child and later on lead to school failure.

The child should be given freedom and should be taught the things, he should not do. If you have to say no sometimes, be in a quiet mood, firm and pointing the things you want him not to do, so that he understands it. You may distract his mind by providing a substitute. This will make him understand as to what is forbidden and what is the meaning of 'no.' Shouting, slapping will curtail his exploratory enthusiasm which parent do not want to lose in the child. One of the method for asking him 'no' is that you hold both the hands of the child and press highly against his cheeks, turn his head towards you. Keep him facing for few seconds and then firmly say 'no' pointing towards the thing, he will understand that the things are not to be touched. But hug him after that. This would avoid punishment and will preserve his exploratory curiosity which is very important for brain development. You might have to do this exercise for sometimes, after which he will know what you really mean. Such situation come when child wants to play with hot press, cup of hot coffee which will injure him or some breakable things.

Common toys at the age of 12 months to 2 years

When child stops putting things in his mouth, he enjoys sand, dough, paints, colouring agents, fitting and plain blocks and puzzles. The recommended toys for this age are:

- Building blocks, balloons

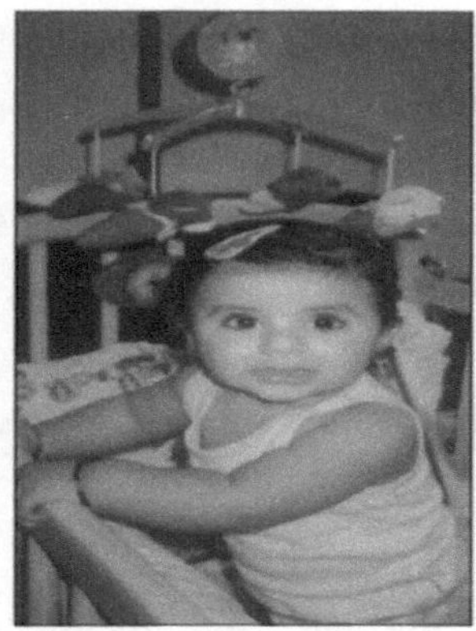 

- Bubbling liquid – to make bubbles

- Paper aeroplanes, paper boats.

- Drawing paper – brush, colour, colour pencils and pens.

- Doughing agents – Plastecine, modeling clay. Light and sound toys – toy gun, toy cars with flash light.

- Peg boards.

Push and pull toys – toy car, wheeled toys. Games like peek a – boo i. e. hiding behind cloth and reappearing is enjoyed very much by the child which he plays with parents and other sibs

At this stage he is associating various words to develop his speech and vocabulary. The child started speaking mama, dada before one year of age. Now his speech is jargon, his own vocabulary is difficult to understand but few words are understandable. At 18 months of age he will speak 10–15 words which will swell to hundred words by 2 years of age. Parents should try to talk with the child whenever they are with him.

Toys of push and pull type are very much enjoyed by child of this age. Toys should be bright but inexpensive. A simple cardboard box may attract attention of the child for hours while expensive toy may not be looked at. Building blocks will inculcate balancing position while balloon gives them idea of air and gravity. Pull and push toys will tell them about application of force. Plasticine, modeling, colouring will develop creativity. Water play (under parent supervision) squeezing toys, animal shapes increase their pleasure.

Stairs fascinate the children very much. It tells children the idea of depth and height. Hide and seek games help children, the concept of stability of surroundings which is not immediately visible and it gives them lot of joy when they discover them. Outdoor trips help them to increase their thoughts. Parents should encourage them to have a feel about birds, trees, grass, flowers, flowing wind, water ponds while at outdoors. It gives children lot of sensory stimuli. Simple outdoor games, running, enjoying various games, eating outside will increase their happiness and intelligence.

Whenever you take your child to shop, show him the fruits, vegetables, bread, chocolates. Give him the idea of hot and cold, show them the different toys available, let them have a feel about them.

Books have their own importance in increasing the intelligence of a small child. Parents should try to read in front of their children. The child often enjoys the picture of toys, animals, human, fruits and vegetables.

Music, songs are enjoyed by children very much, they even dance at soothing or fast tunes. These give children the listening stimulation.

Stimulating Intellectual Growth Eighteen Months to Three Years

12

The child at this age of eighteen months to three years is eager to learn and has insatiable desire to do activities and has enough energy to run faster than most of mothers. **It is often difficult to persuade them for the toilet or going to bed. They act rebellious against the restrictions. The child wants to be independent and wants to do everything himself and resists the "no" – "no" of the parents. At this time if the child is given opportunities to learn and to satisfy his curiosity, he can become more competent for later life.**

(a) Learning

This all needs material, methodology and opportunities to stimulate child's activities, play, speech and develop control over his actions. The more stimuli are given to the child's brain, more intelligent and smart he will become. The more he grows, he needs more sensory and motor stimulation to think, to reason out and to develop speech. He just wants to be happy and perfectionist but according to his development he tries to perform as good as he can. For this, he needs freedom to touch, to manipulate to pull-push, to rearrange, to group, to explore, to throw and to take part in the activity. This all he learns by doing and seeing.

If you impose restriction, upon a child or lecture him for some activity it is not a learning. Learning is what he is acquiring of his own by exploration, experimentation and if he does not succeed, doing it again but parents should be helpful to him for all such activities and not pushing him or pressurizing him.

Since the child repeats his activity again and again to master it, the parents should not get annoyed by child's repetition. In fact, they should take advantage of it because it helps the child to acquire the habit of being expert and neat in his activity.

The child follows and imitates the adult. Try to teach the child in steps, may it be hand wash, throwing ball, holding a racket or setting the table. This is called programmed learning. This will teach the child a necessary skill of the activity. The child likewise could be helped in dressing by himself which would give him immense satisfaction and independence. Remember not to put pressure on the child to learn what he does not want to learn because it will not make him skilled. You can always ask the child if he wants to learn. If he resists and is not interested, ask him again in a friendly manner after some time. In a particular activity, if the child feels bored, put that activity away and offer him that some days later. This will avoid pressure on the child and resistance to your teaching attempts as well. Teach him household items, equipment's, toys etc. Toys help in development of imagination of the child as well as creativity. Animal figures, human figure, painting, doll house, doctor set, kitchen set, cars, trucks, engines and many more are available in the market. Grown up children want to ride tricycle, swings, scooter, bars, sledge, which help them to know about speed activities. These help physical, mental and psychological growth of the child. Art and Craft, computer games, visit to a zoo, trip outside on bus, car, train to sea beach or an orchard make him happy and give him mental stimulation.

(b) Developmental Mile-stones 2 years – 3 years

Age in months	Gross motor	Fine motor	Language & communication	Perception
24 months	Runs well, opens door	Helps to undress	3 words sentence language, listens stories	Turns pages of book. Makes tower of 7 cubes
30 months	Goes up-stairs alternating feet, jumps	Pretends in play	Knows full name	Tower of 9 cubes
36 months	Rides tricycle	Plays simple games, copies line and circles.	Knows age and sex	Makes tower of 10 cubes

(c) Toys & games

2 years – 5 years (pre-school age)

Child recognizes shapes and colours; sounds, and has the sense of rhythm, likes moving objects and sensation of speed.

Suggested toys are:-

- Vehicle – tricycle for speed, balance, slides, swings, car, truck, train
- Story books – for imagination.
- Cutting and pasting works – to encourage creativity and concentration give him blunt scissors, paper
- Use of cassette player, music, rhythm and dancing.
- Balls, bat, rackets.
- Snake-Ladder and carom board.
- Black board

- Plastecine or modelling clay, colouring material and games
- Dolls
- Doctor set
- Kitchen set
- Household items

The child often gives clues for need of learning and you need not to push or impose upon him. Your simple job is to provide opportunities and encouragement.

(d) Language development

Many parents and relatives help the child to acquire speech, correcting the words and praising his efforts to speak. The child often feels confident of the gesture of his parents for their help and he tries to repeat the same word again and again. As already stated that child starts referring ma-ma, da-da, by age of 40 weeks onwards and starts speaking some familiar words at about 15 months which swell to hundred words by two years of age. Some children can participate verbally at the age of 3–4 years. Child also responds to seriously posed questions and communicates his needs and feelings. Some children do not let their parents know what they want. Parents can always make the child understand the rules of discipline, safety to avoid mishappenings. You can help him to learn important words when you are with him and not by forcing him. Body parts, articles of dress, good morning, good evening, hallo, bye-bye, colours, common objects etc. are some of the words, that can be taught at around eighteen months of age. Sometimes the child who is unable to explain what he wants, becomes cryful and irritable. For example he is afraid or a toy and if that toy is kept in the room, he will start crying by just entering the room and may point out at the toy and if that is removed from his sight, he feels happy. So the parents can know by his actions.

(e) Injury

The children do fall sometimes and get injured, even they get some cut and blood may ooz out. The child should be explained about action and accident and the result that can produce. This would explain him the danger of environment and accident which he can avoid. After a minor fall, he may be helped a bit to get up but largely develops his confidence when he manages to get up by himself with appropriate sympathy for the injury.

(f) Discipline and obedience

Discipline means to teach the child what is right and what is wrong, to get along with others, to understand limits and to think of acceptable behavior. Discipline does not mean punishment, shouting or spanking but it is a method to organize the child for later life. Obedience in some cases become absolute and the child should follow the command but should not be over used to stop him from his learning by investigation and experiences. It should only be used in situation which are not for learning or the child may go wrong way.

(g) Simple games and sounds

As you start teaching your child about various colours, you can always ask the child as to what various blue coloured things kept in the room. This will enrich his knowledge about colours or you can ask about the sizes or shapes of the various things around at three years of age. Such question will help the child think about language and shapes and colours. The child should be trained for various sounds also such as flowing of water, electric bell, cell phone, car horn, aeroplane sound, car sound, train sound, siren of a factory etc.

(h) Poems

The child of two and half to three years takes much interest in poetry and nursery rhymes. Whatever their meaning may be. The common rhymes in schools and at home are many such as "Baa-Baa Black Sheep," "Twinkle Twinkle little stars," "Pussy cat." Such poems are available in books or cd's and attract the children very much. By these, children develop memory, rhythm and idea about similar word sounds. Children keep on repeating them and feel pride in telling them to relatives. Such association of language should never be considered as waste of time. The child repeats the poem again and again which is a characteristic of the child at this age. Such repetitions bring him mastery of imagination and language.

(i) Stories

Children while going to sleep prefer stories which are small and may be about animals, birds, sun, moon and about children, the objects which are familiar to them. The children wants to know about the world around. The subject of the stories may be anything which may convey or may not convey any sense but it absorbs the small child, which enlarges the imagination. Often the child goes to sleep while listening to the stories. Children story books are also available.

(j) Books and reading

Children love books very much. Child's pleasure in the books and reading them regularly at sometime, enhance their thoughts and reading skills. They should be encouraged to read regularly. Reading before bed time, relaxes them. Cheaper books may be purchased and habit of reading should be developed in the child. A book library establishment at home, is a good idea where child can choose the book he wants to read. Reading inculcates early learning and eagerness to know about the world around. They learn much by verbal method as well as looking at words and listening to them. At age of three year the child learns counting 1–10 digits. At three years of age, child can be made conversant with the idea that written words are also the language, that are put down on the paper. The children can be taught how words look like. Words like A, B, C or 1, 2, 3 look like and what that means. This would depend upon the child's eagerness to know.

(k) Schooling at 3 years

The objective of school is to satisfy the inherent drive of learning, to give stimuli to develop his mental capabilities, to develop academic characteristics, personality, needs. The parents should choose the school which can give the best.

When to send the child to play school

Normally the child starts participating verbally and develops control of urination and defecation by the age of three years. There is no harm in sending a three years old child for a nursery or play school where he could play and talk to other children. Such school should be in the neighbourhood and should not lay much emphasis on studies.

School reluctance – In preschool age, the child has to be prepared for the school much earlier that he actually starts going. The child who stays at home with parents shall be reluctant to go to school because of fear of separation. The children who play with neighbourhood children, find them self-easy to go to school and adjust there in.

Schoolsmall children

Kindergarten or Playschools – The basic purpose of school is to help youngster to adjust to schools and to give them learning environment. **The most important job in child's life at 3 yrs. of age is to learn, to get along with others and have fun which he learns by interacting with other children of same age group.** It is particularly valuable for that child who lives in small apartments where there is no place to run about or play or who does not get any chance to play with other children or whose both parents work outside home. For such children, a play school is to learn and play with other children.

Nursery schools

Such schools aim at giving the children at age of 3 to 4 years, half to one third of the day under trained teachers. They make the child creative and capable for music, dancing, painting, play, games, modeling and outdoor play and care of dolls. The child develops artistic academic capabilities. Though these school differ enormously in approach but their primary goal is social development. The children get experience of other similar aged children and learns the feelings of others about sharing and being member of the group.

Montessori schools

This concept was developed by a women physician, who by observation and experimentation developed a large series of objects with gradually increasing amount of skill and maturity in a particular task like arranging cubes, matching colors etc. Once the child masters the skills, he is given the next greater amount of task. The child is advanced step by step to learn reading skill and counting starting from 3 years. The school also incorporates cultural and social activities. The child is taught to learn at his own pace in the school. Writing and reading skills are started around 4–5 years of age. The school are considered as partner in child's development. Teacher serves as guide to child's needs. Thus the child gets to develop his mental capabilities and satisfy his inherent drive to learn.

1st day at playschool

It depends on the sensitivity of the children. Those children who are already exposed to outside environment and neighbourhood children adapt the school better than those who are overprotected. If a 3 years old child is left at play school by mother, she may not make fuss right then but after sometime she may start crying by not finding her mother there and may become frightened. The next day she may not like to go to school. Hence the child should be introduced to school gradually. For few days mother might stay near by while the child plays and then takes her home after sometime. Each day the mother may shorten the time of staying there till the child become accustomed to school.

13

Intellectual Growth at Three to Six Years

Three years onwards, a child can ride a tricycle, plays simple games, can copy a line and a circle, knows his age and sex and can make tower of 10 cubes. Around four years, a child can hop on foot, plays with children, can dress and undress himself, can tell a story and can copy square, cross and few alphabets while at five years, he can run down on alternate foot, can wash his face and dries hands, know colours and can draw a triangle.

Growth at 4 to 5 Years

48 months	Hops on one foot	Plays with children, can dress and undress,	Tells a story	Copies cross and square and few alphabets
60 months	Runs, dances, Can skip on alternate foot	Writes few alphabets, draws triangle, square washes face and dries.	Names 4 colours	Draws a triangle

Sanju aged four years is going to school this term and already knows to read independently and can do counting. His speech is fluent without hesitation. He remains curious about his subjects to acquire knowledge. He has many good friends too.

Priya is also four years old. Teacher understands her with little difficulty. The child cannot interpret the book pictures. The child used to remain anxious and quiet and often used to look out through window as she was passing through much of family turmoil. Though child used to go to play school but used to remain alone without playing and making friends.

With the above example you will see that Sanju is smart and intelligent child and remain curious about gaining the knowledge. He shall be ahead of his class fellows and will be absorbed in his profession earlier than his counterparts in later life. While Priya is not curious in her studies and remains aloof due to anxiety. Teachers do not expect much from her. There is lack of interest in the child because of anxiety, deficiency in language and lack of readiness.

There are so many such boys and girls in the school these days. It depends upon the relationship of the child and parents, poverty, undernutrition and presence of diseases in the family. If Priya could have been stimulated like Sanju and the child-parent relationship was very harmoneus, there would have been no anxiety in the child. **Priya could have been stimulated like Sanju and she could have been a smart and intelligent girl. Other few common factors are treatable and can be taken care of. Mental stimulation is important factor which is still to be recognized.**

There should not be a preset and fixed common programme for child stimulation which every parent should follow because parents vary in their talents and time available. Even if programme could be made available, it will not be suitable for children who are physically and mentally so active that it may not suit such a child who will like to learn by his curiosity and eagerness and may not be advantageous to everyone. The thoughts of the child goes to many directions in short span, they are likely to miss the desired teaching opportunities. **The programmes should be directed to need of individual child for which early learning at home is most advantageous.** For this, general guidelines for major areas should be covered between ages of three to six years but its success will depend upon his aptitude of learning, time spent by parents and how much stimulation has already been given to child before three years of age. **Let the child make his own discoveries rather than imposing upon him the fixed lesson and pushing him through. You could give the child, joy of learning. These areas usually are his reading habits, his command on language, his perception (recognition) of particular fact, formation of concepts and his schooling.**

(a) Reading habit

Motivations of a child for reading should done between age of three to four years, which could be done at home and schools which should include sight

of the word, its phonation and way of communication. The child will be fascinated by questions, books, pictures, labels, written holdings and shall add to his vocabulary fast. Commonly, the children with reading difficulties avoid reading or there may lack of reading patience. Consequently, a delay in reading proficiency becomes pronounced. If helped gradually child progresses from single word to sentences and to stories. He also learns to write the letters and then uses the script. Parents can create interest in child by suggesting games for awareness of sound patterns which is basic step in learning to read. Parents can ask the child to speak as many words which resemble "mama" or "dady" Reading should continue to be a pleasure even after elementary school years.

Processing speech in the brain

In this diagram you can see that the words you say start in Wernicke's area, which plans the sounds. The arrows indicate the flow of nerve signals, through Broca's area and finally to the motor cortex.

Which half of your brain is more important?

Both halves of your brain have important functions. Although the 'dominant' hemisphere is more important for language and manual skills, the other half is important for recognizing objects, faces, and music. The left side of the motor cortex controls muscles on the right side of your body, and vice versa.

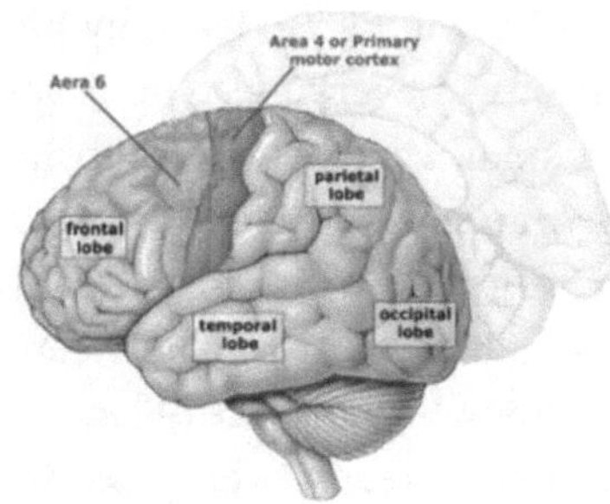

(b) Language

The language is a sort of barometer of recognition and emotional development and involves listening, understanding, talking and writing. As already stated that the most dramatic development in early period is language development. The child often points out with index finger rather than his whole hand for finding out the name of the object. His vocabulary balloons from 10–15 words at 18 months to 100 or more at 2 years of age. A toddlers begins to combine them to make simple sentence such as "give me" "get up" etc. The language development occurs most rapidly between two to five years of age and vocabulary increase from 100 to 2000 words. The sentence structure advances from 2–3 words to full sentence which is both expressive and receptive (understanding). The language acquisition depends upon environment and factors inside the child, family atmosphere and training. Children modify their language progressively. Preschool language development lays the foundation for success in school. Picture books play special role in familiarizing the young child to printed words and also develop verbal language. **Reading aloud with a young child is an interactive process, in which the parents focus the child attention to particular picture, get his response and give the feedback.** Suppose the parents show a picture of a bird to the child and asks"what is this, **the child will say it is a bird. Then parents give feedback "yes, it is a bird." The question, answers and feedbacks are repeated many times during the course of reading, the child sophistication grows and the child's learning increases.**

If the parents speak language correctly, the child will try to learn correct pronunciation. He will pick – up the right words and good language.

This does not mean that you have to speak copy book language with complete sentences every time but use full sentence for your child to learn. The child will learn the subject, pronoun, verb, adjective, tense, singular and plural and clause. The parent can use even little difficult words which the child will absorb gradually. We can further enhance the language in following ways.

1. **Stuttering** – During Speech development, the child may stutter, because of fast thinking by the child and small vocabulary, during which there is process of establishment of brain hemisphere dominance which controls the speech. In a right handed child the speech area is in left hemisphere and in left handed it is right hemisphere of the brain. The stuttering will subside after establishment of speech area in the brain hemisphere but will often persist in the child, in which there is no consistency for right or left handedness and it may start again in attempt to force natural left handed to right handed. Stuttering, that occurs in most of children between two to four years in which extra facial or neck muscle are not working and should be ignored which will almost always disappears. If it persists or a habit is formed, speech

training may be required for correction of speech. Speech therapists are available for such training. The child should think before or take a pause or take deep breath before talking. Give your child time for listening, in which he will not try to speak very fast and will not stutter and will develop self-confidence. Encourage him to plan before talking to avoid mistakes. This way his social behavior will also improve. Television may be helpful in vocabulary development. Visit to zoo, museum or even market would provide new words to your child.

2. **Television, computer, internet and trips** – Television can give lot of information and gives stimulus to discuss the programmes, not only this, it encourages to acquire more information about aeroplanes, outer space, rockets, different sites in the country and news. Television is also helpful in speaking correct language and correct words and increases vocabulary of the child. Internet is good source of information which is ready made source for news, literary or encyclopedia or any other information about different countries. Computer and telephone service is required for internet surfing. You can always talk to the child in a happy way, talking with person outside are country, jobs or puzzles and rhymes are enjoyed very much by the children. Such talks develop intimacy and learning through language. Regular trips to either museum, zoo or market help the child to learn many new things. Name of animals, names of equipment's, name of surroundings objects increase their vocabulary and language.

3. **Library – A regular trip to library should be made routine for the child after four years of age. The child can choose book of his own choice and get pleasure out of it.** If possible make a bookshelf of child of his own at home. This would also increase his interest in the books and information. Make reading a pleasure. Books for preschool children are available in the market. These may be story book, fairy tales, about geographical and science phenomena such as clouds, rain, lightening or thunder, magnet, electricity traffic signals, labels and various printed letters. The book should match the mental level of the child so that he could read or listen with ease. Poetry also interests the child very much at five or six years of age. Encourage your child to memorize and enjoy the rhymes which may be repeated as often as required. The child often feels pleasure in such reciting.

4. **Second language development** – The child at the age of three to six year has greater ability to learns the second language, if given an opportunity. He just needs to hear it spoken. If the parents, school teacher, neighbours speak the second language to the child in the house or school, the child gradually learns the language. Correctness in speech is important. Such language development can also be helped by books. Children learn second language quicker than adults.

(c) Perception

Perception mean knowledge which is achieved by ability to transmit stimuli to the brain and interpreting them. It may be voice of the mother, sun being hot or photo representing reality. Perception is perceived by all human senses such as seeing, hearing, smelling, tasting, touching. Out of these seeing and hearing are most important for learning. These stimuli pass along the concerned nerves to brain centres for interpretation and recognition. If the things are wrongly interpreted it can cause great difficulty in normal life for recognition of the object such as difference in pen and pencil, a snake or a rope, right and left etc.

The cause of such misperception may be brain injury around birth or during maturation of brain. In such case child may be irritable, clumpy, overactive, with short attention span (Minimal brain damage syndrome) and poor concentration, anxious or impulsive. For such children special training is required before schooling such play therapy, recognition practice of various things. Setting up of obstacles and following the route by running, crawling or jumping, balancing of body and objects, identification of left and right, teaching of shapes (squares, circle, oval, rectangle, cone) simple designing, finding missing parts in two almost similar pictures, encourage talking after showing picture, describing a trip to grossery, playground or other places. Recitation of similar sounding words. Etc.

For such training, help of psychiatrist, pediatrician or a school teacher for special training may be required which will improve the activity, concentration span and behavior problem of the children. It is better to train such children before they go to school.

The child's perception should be enhanced in subjects of mathematics and various science subjects even they may be good at these.

1. **Mathematics** – The child will be greatly benefited by school teaching if he already has the perception of mathematical skills which he can

get from games and numbers. Teaching basic concepts, building on them and expanding them are important. The subject should be made interesting even if child is good at it.

The child be taught about counting from 0–9 or more, Big letters may be used for such teaching. The child may be given idea of odd and even by numbers cards. He should be given to know about zero (0) which means 'none' but how the words and their meaning changes after putting zero on their right side. "Idea of "same" or "equal" by two identical numeral will make him understand the concept. Similarly adding and subtraction by increasing and removing the number card may be given. Give your child the concept of ones, tens, hundred and thousands also.

Dice may be very helpful for children to learn about number game of adding and subtraction. The child should work without any pressure. This way he will get absorbed to win. Once the child learns to read and write the number, it is not difficult to teach him reading time on the clock or to read thermometer or counting money.

2. **Science** – The child has insatiable interest in exploring the world around which should be respected and encouraged. The child should not be pressurized to memorize the facts but his questions should be answered and be encouraged to make observations.

   The parents can always make the child sensitive about the environment. He may be taken to parks and be shown the tender shoots of green trees, flowers and their fragrance, running water producing sound, flow of air, birds of various colours, feels of grass and dew. Taking him to see the river, its flow and boats floating in the water. He can also be taken to sea-shore showing him waves in water, children playing, feel of sand, chirping of birds, fish, shells, ships, rising of sun. Take him to agricultural fields, to show green fruit trees, tube well, ponds, animals, a cart, pond, well, irrigation, canals, tractor, ploughing and how seeds grow. Seeds for growing do not require sun while plants require it. The child should know about the nature physical phenomenon such as day, night, wind, rains, moon, stars, sun, heat, cold, clouds and lightening etc.

   He can be taken to a shopping trip showing him decoration of shops, flowers and their fragrance, shapes and colours, people purchasing various house hold items, lighting, travelling, machines such as bicycle, scooter, bus, train, aeroplane. The parents job should not be just to teach the names of what child loves at but also share and create interest in the child so that he asks questions to know more. Try to answer the child's question as it comes. If you choose to postpone his queries due to some emergency situation, take initiative of telling answers yourself later on. If you do not know the answer, tell your child that you do not know and you can find the answer together. Teach your child, the source of gathering the information which may be internet, library, encyclopedia. You should look up the answer and inform the child. Similarly, science museum may also be visited where child can learn about earth, sun, moon and various orbits encircling around the sun.

At home, you can show the child a refrigerator, freezing of water into ice and melting of ice into water. You can also showing your child boiling water and the steam coming out of it to give the idea of boiling, cloud formation and steam engine.

Show him the dropper, how do we fill it with medicine or water?, show him teaspoon or tablespoon, food we eat, colours we use. What happens when we add sugar or salt to the water and the way it dissolves. Show him the evaporation of water while you put cloths in the sun for drying. Demonstrate the condensation on the mirror in bathroom when do we use warm water while taking bath. Toys, play-things, magnet, lenses, mirror, clock, prism may also be included in child's experience.

Tell your child about sounds such as chirping of birth, flow of water and wind, playing children, sound vibrations, playing of tape, music, door-bell, moving wheels, sound of car and bus, sound of mill, siren or train whistle. How the sound travels? About telephone, and if you talk with long plastic pipe and other child listening at the other end.

(d) Concept formation

Once the child perceives, the information that is, the sensory stimuli reach the brain and interpreted, the ideas are formed. The Child is constantly reorganizing the sensory stimuli and perceptions to understand and have ideas about the world around him.

The child wants to learn about past, geography, and science which help him understanding daily life, because of craving for understanding in developing mind. A few nursery schools and kindergartens have understood the need of new type of teaching methods for these children to discover and make the concepts. The role of parents should be, to give the child an accurate concept. They should listen to the child and should understand the information which may be correct or wrong. This information should be corrected and given to the child. For example when child after visiting a farm will make the concept that seeds are sown in the land, water is given, the seed grows and turns into plant, or tree, it gives fruits, that are sent to market from where we purchase them for our use. Similarly, the parent help the children to know about grocers shop where the things come from far distances, we purchase them by money which is determined by the grocer and the money we get from where we work. Children have lots of misconception about the parents work. The child knows that his mother and father go for work to bring money but they do not understand the type of jobs. You can make the child understand about.

The jobs are such as policeman, doctor, nurse, salesman, factory worker, a driver and the relation of his work to the community welfare.

A trip by bus gives the child the idea of transportation which carries from one place to another. The child should know that there are various kind of transportation – bicycle, rickshaw, scooter, car, bus, train, planes, rockets, hot air balloons, horses, helicopter, trams, boat, ships. Their uses should be told to children. Which of them carry the persons by air, land and water and how they run.

The child should be give the idea of time – seconds, minutes, hours, days, week, months and years. This could be explained by drawing big circle which represents one year. Divide the circle into twelve segments which indicate months. Each segment is divided into four which depict weeks, similarly days and hours can be described. Use of clock will show seconds, minutes and hours.

Maps represent the land area and its relationship to around. It also shows water, mountains, winds and temperature etc. Time and direction of a country can be known from longitude and atmosphere by latitude lines. Equator line represent very warm areas while poles are coolest. You can ask your child to map the living room locating the beds, chair, window, bathroom, storing space and doors. Give him the concept of scale on bigger paper showing relationship of your house with neighbourhood. Similarly map of city, state, country and world can be made to understand.

Similarly the child can be given concept of solar system. He may be taken to planetarium to show how we live on earth and what is its relationship to

Sun, Moon and other orbits. How all orbits move around? How day and night occur? How solar and lunar eclipses take place?

The child should be told about family relationship – mother, father, grand-parents, brother, sister, cousins and close relationships and friends. The concept of marriage, sex should be explained to them. Manners are equally important. Why a child requires manners and behavior to remain nice and popular in society.

There are many more things which are beyond description in this book are about human relationship, friendship, history, social behavior and lot more, can be discussed with the child from time to time. The child will make concepts based on his observations. The child often enacts them with his friends and learns by them. These concept become clear more so year by year when the child grows. Parents help make future learning more efficient.

(e) Toys

Children between age of three to six years enjoy to play with toys. Many of the toys which are enjoyed between the age of eighteen months to three years are still enjoyed at age of three to six years which have been described in appropriate sections and should also include musical instruments such as drums, record player, bells, sitar, flute, xylo phones. Dramatic plays including costumes, masks, puppets, wings and warfare equipments. Physical play equipment such as swings, wheelbarrow, tricycle, balls, climbing apparatus, tunnels, seats and merry go around. Puzzles, colour matching, peg Boards, Carrom Board, Magnet, Prisms, Magnifying glass.

(f) Regular schooling

"It is impossible to win the race unless you venture to run, impossible to win the victory unless you dare to battle"

– Richard M. Devos

Are you a victor or a victim? The victims may never achieve their goals. But if we see ourselves as victors and use given abilities and talent, we will be victors. The smallest one among us can slay the greatest giant with right attitude, hence learning the right attitude is important for which school is the right place. Customary early school years are 6–12 years. This period is also known as middle childhood, while preschool age is 2–5 years. The school age children have the power of perception to evaluate themselves in school.

Healthy development of a child requires increasing separation from parents and opportunities to negotiate challenges in outside work. The child functions at home, school and neighbourhood. Hence school is important destination where child learns to get along with the people and prepares himself for an adulthood. Of course along with this, child learns to read, write and knows mathematics skills and other subjects which show him the way to progress. In school the child comes in contact with different groups of children and he shares his experience with them. Thus the school is a foundation for his future.

School reluctance

When the study load rises along with the complexity of subjects, the child is not able to understand the contents. The goal of writing becomes composition and not just the spelling. Some children are not able to cope up with the complexity and try to avoid school. Initially on pretext of illness, he does not go to school and then observes prolonged absence from school to avoid punishment from teacher. Such children develop psychological problems like vomiting, headache or abdominal pain or giddiness. Sometimes such a child does not get well along with others. Other children tease him and then he tends to avoid school. The mother should not show overprotection and may deal with moderate strictness. She may take advice of a psychologist or psychotherapist.

Choice of regular school

Apart from looking at the results in the school examinations, parents have to look at many other points for overall development of the child. The school building, type of students, economic status, status of teachers and their interest in child's growth, character building, general knowledge and behaviour of children and teacher and child relationship. Games and other skilled activities are also important besides the studies. If the school is in close vicinity, it would certainly be better for the child and would save lot of journey time.

School education medium such as English, Hindi or regional language is important aspect of imparting education. Co-education school for younger children help to develop balanced inter-personal relationship.

Frequent changing of school by child should not be encouraged. It makes child's adjustment difficult and studies to suffer. Boarding school may be good for those children whose parents are frequently transferred from one place to another, like foreign services or army or the children who are unable to devote time to studies at home.

Younger children require warmth and security of parents and should not be sent to boarding school for the sake of punishment, the child should never be sent to boarding school, such children develop hostile attitude in life and the difficulty with family adjustments.

Scholastic performance

Child's school performance is affected by number of factors.

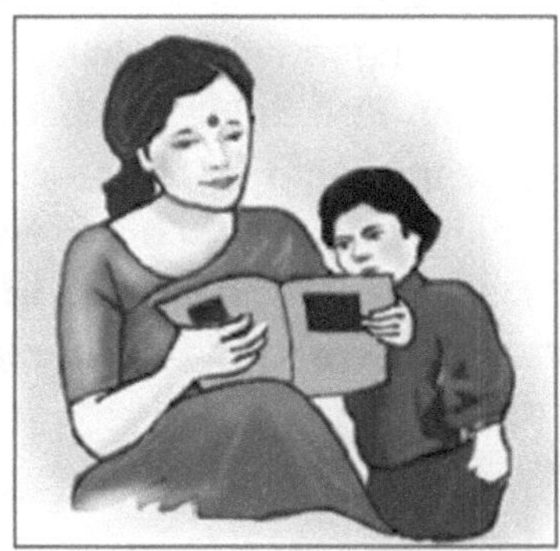

Studying

1. Overzealous parents who want their children to do the best in the class and if the children are unable to do that, they are punished or nagged. Sometimes parents also want their children to be promoted to next class even if they are unable to perform fair in their class.

2. The children who have been put to school too early are unable to compete with their older counterparts. Such children do poor in the school.

3. Disharmony among the family member lead to difficulty in adjustment and anxiety. Loss of love and care also causes poor performance in school.

4. Prolonged illness of the child, missed school days or handicapped children with reading and writing difficulties also make poor performances in the school.

Parent-child-teacher relationship

Parents should take active interest in school activities and performances of the child and also should find out the relationship of their wards with teachers and other children. Schools have parent-teacher meeting which should be attended by the parents. They should discuss about the progress/problems of the child.

Competitive spirit

The parents should try to improve competitive spirit in their children. These are the days of competition and to take up any profession, the child has to pass through competition.

Parents should encourage the children to do their home work regularly. Parents should help the children to cope up with the challenge and not to increase their fear psychosis for examination. Few children under such condition develop examination phobia and are unable to perform well in examination due to forgetfulness. **Medicines should not be used for awakening at night since such medicines would cause mental exhaustion in children. Helping the child to solve difficulties by extra coaching, encouragement and care would go long way with examination.**

Managing studies

Few children feel that they find it very difficult to study at home after school hours because there are many things to do at home. These things include playing, watching TV, phone calls from fellow students, fellow parties, home jobs, helping parents for routine works, rest, meals, tuitions and then home work is to be done which is difficult to complete. After school hours, they are left with little time of 4–5 hours, so it becomes difficult to manage everything and specially their studies.

We have talked to our education experts about the study management problem and according to them the students must obey some simple rules which are as follows.

1) Time management

Student should learn to manage his time. He should divide his time into five parts as follows

- Time to communicate with parents and help them and other family members.

- **School work/self study.**

- **Play /hobby/going out.**

- **Personal** – TV watching, talking to friends or relatives on phone or directly, newspaper reading.

- **Introspection** – he should plan his next day and think about as to how much he has already achieved?

He should make time table keeping in view of above programmes and follow them strictly. The student should learn to say "No" if it does not fit with his time table and also he should not be dependent on his parents for the study. He must be self-dependent.

2) Fixing priorities of your time table

The most important work should be done first of all and it should be at the top of your time table, like school homework and rest of things should follow depending upon your priorities. This way you will feel satisfaction and will have no anxiety about your school work.

3) Make timetable of your study

Since you have fixed your priorities in which you might have put school homework and study in the first place.

Self Study

Then you must also put which home work is to be done or to study first of all maths, science or others? This way you do not waste your time in thinking, what to do first?

4) Anticipate the studies

You already have the knowledge that you have to appear in competitive examinations, school examinations or class tests and also to attend to your parties and your community programmes. Then try to adjust the studies accordingly so that there is no loss of your studies.

In this way the student shall be able to cope up with their studies and shall stand at a better place as compared to other fellow students in all spheres of life.

How to study?

This was also a question in front of our education experts. Few children mug up the subject, few make the notes, few keep on underlining the book, some of them keep on writing on the margins of the book and so on. But they may be finding difficulty while writing in examinations. Few children complain that they remembered everything but on the day of examination they forgot everything, which may be due to being over anxious.

(i) To study in school

The student has to study according to the school time table. He must interact with his teacher to clear his doubts. This can be further enforced if the student has read the subject previous evening at home. The child should anticipate the competitive or other examinations. He must prepare himself from day one and not just during last 2 to 3 months before examination. If he chooses to study only during last days of examinations then he becomes overanxious and is likely to forget all what he has learnt and will not be able to do well in examination. On the contrary, if he is studying from day one, he becomes confident and shall do well in examination.

(ii) At home

The child should follow his time table strictly and should avoid other jobs which come in between his programme. While learning he must study a paragraph and should understand paragraph. What message has been given by writer in that paragraph. Next he should close his eyes and try to recall the facts in points, written in that paragraph text. After which he should write the points, he recalled. In between he should not open the book and look back. If he recalls about 80% of what he has read, he should proceed to next paragraph otherwise he should repeat the same again with same procedure and so on. This would make him confident in his studies. Parents must check the home work or study of their child at night. Try to improve the pronunciation by asking him to read loudly, by talking to him in a clear understandable way. The child can also be helped for pronunciation. He can do it by watching news reader in television programmes or listening to radio. Ask the child to read at least one paragraph from newspaper and select any five words from there everyday. Those selected words, he should write in a note book, finding their meaning in dictionary and using them in sentences. In this way he will develop a good vocabulary and command on language very fast.

Should the Child of Preschool Age (3–5 Years) Be Taught to Read?   14

In late 1950, many researches were made about teaching under five years of age. In early part of twentieth century, substantial number of children were unable to read. It was thought, since the reading is a complicated process, the parents might use wrong method to teach a child which may put pressure over a child and make him emotionally disturbed. It was also thought that it was difficult to make the child learn until his mental age is over five to seven year. After which series of researches appeared and it was decided that it is good to help the child for reading as he will help learning himself by asking questions at the age of five to five and a half years of age. Later it was seen that child who comes to school, if already reading, learned the subject spontaneously. Researches to date show that child will gain much and loose nothing whatever the parent teach him, will help him. But they should not try to teach reading unless the child enjoys the process. Reading is now being thought to three and four years old children. In Denver state school, researches suggests that average child should be about four and a half years old to get profit in reading though youngster with special aptitude and interest could begin earlier, at about three. **Dr. Fowler thinks that the child of four years has mental age to read, though he had successfully taught children at three.**

The girls are more interested in reading and read happily and fluently above their age level.

Those children who can read at preschool age get head start and maintain his advantage all through elementary school. His IQ is likely to be increased permanently. No learning problems result from earlier start in reading, is suggested by long term studies in Denver USA in 1960, in which 4000 youngster were followed up from kindergarten to ten years of age. There was no harmful or social affect seen in the results including school adjustment, reading or disliking for reading or vision. Early reading had many positive advantage when children were given opportunity to move ahead in the school. These children had significant higher reading rates and had larger vocabulary than traditionally programmed children. Early reading children were better in comprehension and scored higher in study skills, mathematics, concepts, language, social studies and science as well. In schools, such pupils in all ability groups benefit proportionately and have lasting effects of programmes to adjusted for advantage. However in America Denver researches also found a young child cannot see letters well enough to read. According to Dr. J.H. Shaw an eye surgeon says that the children can focus and accommodate at even one year of age and can read at an early age. Few researcher felt that teaching at early age will rob him of his childhood and would prevent social and emotional growth but **according to Denver school reading programme, which advocates that youngster can make significant progress if parents spent only thirty minutes per week with the child and it will not have any bad effect on social and emotional growth but will have larger gain in later life.**

Do not drag the child to make him learn so much every day, also do not try to teach reading until he is enjoying it. Do not attach any penalty for his not learning if he is not in a mood to learn. Stop minutes before he seems restless or bored. Do read to your child happily, lovingly and frequently for about sixty minutes per week. Give your child love of reading which is the best assurance he will keep in future. The parents should use reading material of large size type. If the child enjoys making reading as a game in school he will be most benefited. When you read to him, just cuddle him close. Show him new sounds, new words. Be enthusiastic about what he remembers and also tell him politely what he has forgotten. Give him happy hug before he leaves you which may just be a ten minutes session. This will keep him and yourself happy. The more you expose him to printed words, the quicker and easier he will learn. Buy him some books to make his own library but do not forget to make a stop at local library with your child regularly and let him choose his own reading material.

Today it is felt that preschool children can be taught to read in happy and successful ways. **Montessori schools feel that children can learn to read more easily at age of four years onwards.** The child is given simple picture cards lined up in a row and then child locates a single word one by one. Suppose he has a picture of "girl." He will repeat the word "g" and will go to open the rack and will bring out a coloured cut word of carboard 'g' and put it near the picture. Likewise he will do one by one for other pictures.

After successfully, mastering the words, he will start combining the word "m" "a" "n" as man and so on. Similarly more of the pictures and names are spelt out by the child. De Montessori discovered that a preschool child could learn and write with enormous enthusiasm. Her text books have been published and is a rich source of study even for culturally deprived children. **A child in Montessori School learn to write before he learns to read.** The child learns to control muscles of his hand for writing with a pencil then he learns the sounds of these letters. The child feels lot of excitement if he could write a letter or learned the sound of the letter. The child should be taught reading by sounding out the word phonetically, then repeating them until understanding. **A four years old usually takes one to one and a half month to achieve his first written word and from writing to reading takes about two weeks.**

These days computers have solved lot of problems of teaching. Software are available to teach the child, a written word and how it sounds by a click of a button. When introduced to a child he will never refuse his turn. The computer will print a single large sized letter on the monitor and will call its name.

In second phase, the computer pronounces the different letters which will make small word, starting from left to right sequences. From such words, the typing goes to sentence. Half an hour session is sufficient. After 46 sessions (18–24 hours) children usually can recognize the letters. This will improves their speech also. Computers would stimulate minds of culturally deprived youngsters of average intelligence.

Dr. Moore and Dr. Montessori have taken great precautions against pressure for reading, on the child. **The child's reward is joy of discovery and feeling of accomplishment by sounding or writing a word.** The children take intensive interest and put lot of concentration by using cardboard words and computer.

For small children, Doman – Delicate method of teaching is used. In this method large sized card with red lettering, two inches high is shown to the child by loving parents. The child is told phonetically the sound of the word. Next time, he is handed the card and asked about the word. If the child tells it correct, he is given a big hug by father and mother and if he does not remember, he is seemly told about what it was.

Every method requires much repetition of words and sounds. Two, three and four years old enjoys repetition but may become boring for a six years old. The child should never be pushed.

15 — Encourage Your Child to Be Creative

Gaurav was only five year old when he went to attend a marriage where some marriage preparation were going on and tents were being erected. Gaurav was giving them very positive alternatives for tent erection.

Prashant was two years old when he was told that the cooker was hot, he should not touch that. After an hour or so he went near by it and hesitantly extended his foot to touch it to feel its heat. At that time it was cold then he touched and played with his hands for more than an hour.

Shreya, three years kept awake whole night and went out frequently to see where does night go before morning? Where does moon go before sun rise? She always felt that night falls, outside the house.

All of the children gave evidence of their creative thoughts.

So creativity means positive creation and adventuring thinking which is a component of intelligence. Dr. Guilford of California has identified many separate intellectual talents but usual types of IQ measures only six to eight elements. The ability to invent original ideas, to formulate concepts and to seek answers to the problems. Such children have higher intelligence. The intelligence may be in science or other fields which may be seen by experimentation and exploration.

Normally IQ is tested in academic areas and research have been made in school aged children but few facts have come to light that the child's creativity begin to increase at 3 years of age and maximize at four and half years and then it decreases. Creativity can be increased by encouraging and training the child. Almost every normal child possesses some creativity which needs to be polished but a wrong training or coercive home practices can make the child less creative.

(a) How do we recognize creativity?

These creative children are quite curious to know the things. They prefer experimentation, which will be clear by following examples.

Sonu was five years old. He was told that if a coin was beaten to made flat it becomes a magnate. To confirm the fact, he went to near by railway line, where he stayed, put the coin on the railway track and stayed many yards away from the track. After one hour of waiting, the train came and flattened the coin. He tested the coin which did not become the magnate. This way he confirmed that coin when flattened does not become magnate.

Such children question constantly to know from the parents or teachers and enjoy them. Such children do not get satisfied with very simple answers and are very sensitive to whatever is happening around. They are always happy to learn. They put such question which are difficult to answer such as if two Gods quarrel with each others, who will win. This is real difficult to answer. Their imagination is active and delightful.

A creative child, five years old in a village got a thin branch of a tree, to which he tied a string to make a bow and arrow for his friend for a festival.

If you ask such a creative child that what are the uses of paper apart from writing on it, he will tell more than twenty uses. Creative children have organizing talent. They organize their own and their friends, birth days in different manners by giving presents and hugs to each other. They have love for pets, cuddling puppies, feeding parrots, loving rabbits and they enjoy them. If you go to their rooms, you may find pictures of their friend, great persons, stuck on the walls. There may be a collection of books, music instrument and balls, rackets for play activity.

Such children attempt different task with ease and consider failures as part of the job and life, instead of getting frustrated. There concentration on a particular task is often more than usual. They find the ways of doing things. If one attempt does not succeed, they find other way to do it and show flexibility in their creation. A creative child is more resourceful and stable and independent thinker. The creative girls are often more powerful than their classmates, show their talent in their respective fields later and prefer to work by themselves. We are reminded of a little girl of three year when she broke some thing or was uncomfortable with some familiar reply. She use to go a table, kept in different room and used to sit there for few minutes and came to pacify the family member. This is the creativity of that girl.

She had adopted to solve the situation instead of crying.

b) Encouraging creativity

As already mentioned in the previous text that the child perceives the things by seeing, hearing, touching, manipulating, smelling, exploring, tasting, climbing and trying. After perceiving they conceive the idea and by pondering that idea they become creative and the creativity grows gradually. Many researches are still going on for this subject. The Parents should help their children to be more creative, may be guided by following few recommendations.

- The child should be given the freedom to express himself. The parents who laugh it off or push off, damage the thoughts of the child. They should explain the pros and cones of the subject instead of pushing that off.

- Involve your child to plan family activities.

- Make the child important and find satisfaction in expression of his feelings.

- Let the child realise that his ideas have the values.

- Stimulate your child to make friends.

- Stimulate your child to venture a project. Creative persons such as scientist, writer and artists have always taken up difficult tasks to become creative famous.

- Make your child to think of the need of day such as what would you do if you see someone injured in front of you?

- Help your child to become an achiever in life.

- School activities – Such as science exhibition gives excellent opportunities for experimentation. Children should be stimulated to take part in that. Motivate him for innovations.

- Allow children to learn their own by experience also. Failure is part of life and children learn from it.

- Recognise his creative efforts. Do not discourage.

- Ask them various used of a particular thing such as brick, paper, TV etc. This will increase their thoughts.

- Take him to various places such as outside trips, to show museum, garden, monuments, exhibition and zoo or at picnic. Then ask them their description.

- Give them some quieter place to study and work.

- Do not interrupt them while they are at work seriously.

- Provide them material for innovation such as pictures, plasticine, papers, playing material, toys, coloured pencils, cloth etc.

- Reward them by praise for their success.

- An imaginative child will play imagination games. Help him in imagination. Such as word building from single alphabets.

- Do not teach everything in much detailed steps, may damage his imagination. Let him think, make imagination and work it out but you can always make suggestions to help him.

- Show your children to make paper boats, how they float on the water? Teach them to make paper airplane, how it flies in air? Show them how to paint water, hills, trees, sun, human figure, grass, birds and how to make 3D pictures. Develop their artistic touch.

- Show if they could make sculpture out of clay.

- Let them make some melodeous music. Some children can begin having some lessons at age of three or four years, i. e., dance, drama, music, instrument training.

- Teach them about outdoor games.

Encouraging you child creatively would give you a delightful pleasure and such creativity should be established before start of school age. A good teacher shall be very helpful to develop it.

A Baby Doctor

How Montessori Ideas Can Stimulate Child's Creativity at Home? 16

As mentioned before, Dr. Maria Montessori was an Italian physician, who laid some basic principles of child stimulation for learning in early 1900s. Her ideas and techniques are successfully practised even today. She put some practical ways of preschool teaching methods. For Montessori schools, she developed child size furniture, wooden puzzles, educational toys, instructions for teaching and other equipment which are applicable in present days nursery schools as well.

As you know, the child at preschool age has great desire to learn, to read, to write and doing the things independently. The years between the age of three to six, the brain of child is developing fast and has the capacity to absorb most easily. Keeping these facts in views Dr. Montessori formulated the basic principles of learning i. e. ideas, technique and equipment which became popular. But there are views against it also. Many nursery teachers do not agree with the technique of implementation, who feel that art and music and other creative activities should be part of the curriculum. The freedom to work as learning task of child's own choice has not been accepted by them. Montessori method differ lot from nursery school methods.

The Montessori teacher called "directress." Her function is to answer the question that child poses and guide the child for self-training without being disturbed. They do not impose learning but try to stimulate the child for that, so that the child feels satisfaction over his accomplishment. The child is praised for work which becomes his motivation for achievement in life.

In Montessori schools, the learning is independent and not in groups. The child works at his own speed and in his own way. The material for work also is chosen according to his ability and interest of the child. There is no competition among his mates nor he is pushed in any way to finish fast. The children work for practical activities such as cleaning the table, pouring the water into a bottle without spilling over, hanging of shirt on a hanger, arranging the beads for numbering, making maps, inlaying of wooden puzzles, making block tower etc. Once the child becomes master of the job by self learning, self correction, understanding right or wrong, he gets another job to do. This way the child will smile with satisfaction of accomplishment. The silence game is also practiced. How to keep silence for two minutes with closed eyes and being motionless. How to move the chair without making noise. This will develop their better hearing and their self control. Thus such activities encourage the child for learning.

Many of Montessori activities can be practiced at home. The ideas and techniques to work can be adopted for the guidelines.

The parents should plan the programmes for the new activity of their preschool child.

- Show your child to handle the material in a slow motion, explaining to him, for example use of pencil to draw line, use of scissors, so that child could see, grasp and conceive the task. If possible, break the task into small steps.

- Let the child do the task himself and the working place should be congenial.

- The task should of child's choice and in no case, the speed should come in the way. The child should do it at his own pace knowing right and wrong aspects.

- If the task does not interest the child, do not insist for doing it.

- While the child is concentrating on the job, try not to interrupt him.

- Show him the environmental phenomenon – hot, cold, rain, clouds, thunder.

- Ensure discipline but in an interesting way such as sitting without making noise or closing the door slowly.

- If the child has not understood the job, show him the easy way so that he does not feel frustrated.

- Let the child learn the exact names of the objects such as colours, objects etc.

- Develop the child's motor skills, such as running, hopping on one foot, handling of glass full of water without spilling, balancing, walking on a line etc.

- Teach him various sounds such as of a particular bird or animal, flow of water, filling of a drum, sound of flowing wind, crunching of paper, sound of a bell, horn of a car, wistle of train etc.

- Develop various feels of different objects like floor, cloth, leather, wood, metal etc.

- Try various odours. Let the child learn various smells, good or bad, fragrance of rose etc.

- Let the child know various tastes, sweet, saltish, bitter, sour.

- Try memory games of matching colours, uses of various objects etc.

- Use picture cards of animal and environment and let the child match them such as cow with grass, lightening with clouds etc.

- Show them various shapes, such as cylinder, cone, round, rectangular etc, and tell their names.

- Raising intelligence – means raising book smartness and environmental (street) smartness.

- It is very important to be armed with street smartness because it is question of survival. One cannot be solely educated on just reading or just you live with, so one needs a combination of street smartness and book smartness – an intelligence.

- The knowledge of theories, laws and concepts open the doors of better opportunities.

How Single Parent Can Make Child Intelligent and Smart?

Though it is normal but little difficult for single parent to bring up a child to meet his or her emotional needs that were being looked after by a former spouse but children need to go with their own emotional growth and development. No child can take the role of an adult. Single parent have to learn to deal with surprised and awkward situations.

The child may loose mother or father because of death or divorce or born to single mother or adopted by single woman. It certainly makes the differences on the psychology of the child by not having mother or father. But if the parent handle the situation cautiously, the child, a boy or a girl, can continue to grow up and get adjusted. An adjusted child is often an intelligent child. To make the child intelligent and smart, the parent's spirit is most important. Though single parent sometimes feels lonely and crossed at times and may take it out on the child who has lost one of the parent. The important thing will be that the parent should go on as a normal human being, keeping reactions or outside carrier active or before. The parent should take the child to his or her friend's or relative's house, or to some picnic, zoo, museum, some historical places, or give the child a stimulus of creativity of environment, art and music will be more valuable for development of the child rather than parent keeping his own routine perfect. As the child grows he will be friendly to someone else to take the place of lost parent. For small children around age of 2–3 years, a kind companionship with other parent is important. Grandfather, uncle, aunt, cousins, school teacher or a combination can show the substitute for normal growth of a small child, if they enjoy the child's company. Children above three years of age or over build up an image of father or mother as their ideal inspiration, whether they remember them or not. Sending the child to cousins place, picking the child from school or encouraging the child to make friends and playing games makes the difference for psychological development of the child. Getting the child into particular hobbies and spiritual companionship may also make the child world appealing. The single parent can make the plenty of fun and should share the interest rather than keeping the child aloof. Single parent should invite the child's friends to their house regularly, will boost confidence in them and will make them smart and intelligent. If the parent continue giving and show hatred towards the child the result will be disastrous. The child under such circumstances may develop bad behaviour, uninterested in studies and indulge in school reluctance and even running away from home.

<table><tr><td>**18**</td><td># Medicines and Their Role in Enhancing Intelligence</td></tr></table>

Certain medicines have been developed for use in loss of memory and brain disorders. These are called cognition enhances or cerebroactive drugs. These medicines do have some effects over brain by various mechanisms but their benefits are uncertain. These medicines have been tested to increase blood flow of the brain to increase the nutrition of the brain neurons which are the basic units of brain. The health of brain depends upon the health of its neurons.

Such medicines are thought to be helpful in memory loss (Alzheimer disease) in old age, mental retardation in children, learning defects, attention deficit disorders, brain stroke, head injury, and electro convulsive therapy (ECT).

Not much of researches have been made in trial of these medicines but since these medicine increases blood circulation of the brain, it is assumed that these medicines might be enhancing intelligence of the child as well and are being prescribed by the medical professionals for disease. However it has been shown that the claims of enhancement of intelligence may just be a wishful thinking of patient relatives and the medical professions. It is also possible that such medicines may divert the blood flow to area which have already increased blood supply, stealing the blood from brain areas which are already deficient of blood, thus may worsen the problem. It is called steal phenomenon.

However if we consider the positive effects of the drugs, usually these are used for increasing blood flow, direct support to neuron, thus improving neural integration and enhancement of memory. Since these medicines are given to children for long time to have their affect it is difficult to differentiate whatever positive affects these medicine have, from the affect of surrounding positive family atmosphere during that period.

These drugs have been classified as under depending upon their action over the brain.

a. **Cognition enhancers** – Piracetam drug in thought to increase the learning and the memory, facilitates the information transfer and increase adenosine triphosphate (ATP) and adenosine diphoshate

(ADP) rates, which give energy to the brain cells. Hence the drug is used in mental retardation, neuron disfunctions, brain surgery, memory impairment, after electroconvulsive therapy and giddiness.

b. **Metabolic enhances** – These drugs increase the blood flow of the brain, thus protecting the brain metabolism. But their useful effect is minor. The group includes hydergine, nicergoline and piribedil.

c. **Cholinergic activators** – Tacrine drug has been used for memory enhancement in old age. Though drug is effective in improving memory, attention and language but its action is of short duration.

d. **Vasoactive Cerebral protectors** – Pyritinol and Ginkgo biloba drugs are thought to counteract decrease in brain blood flow and improve cognitive brain functions by increasing glucose transport to the brain providing energy to the brain cells. Hence these are recommended in head injury, prolonged anesthesia, delayed milestones in infants, for improving concentration and memory and organic brain problems.

However the extent of usefulness is uncertain. Encephabol (pyritinol) and ginkoba (ginkgo bilobe) are available on preparation.

Role of vitamins

Many parents seek opinion from the child specialist regarding improvement of their child's memory and ask to prescribe some vitamin pills for this. Some of the medical professionals believe that vitamins have positive effect over improvement of memory. Researches have proved that there is no scientific proof of additional vitamin supplements in improvement of memory but the vitamins normally be obtained from balanced diet for general growth of the body as a whole.

Q. 1. Can we raise the intelligence of a child?

Ans. Yes – The child does not have a fixed intelligence. It is changeable to better or worse by his environment during early years of life. If we provide him suitable home environment, school environment and social activities, we can raise his intelligence. The critical years for development of intelligence are up to six to eight years.

Q. 2. What do you mean by wisdom?

Ans. Wisdom is the ability to make sound chores and good decisions. **It is an intelligence shaped by experience** where there is profound understanding and deep insight of the subject.

Q. 3. How do we recognize the creativity of the child?

- Creative children are very sensitive to whatever is happening around.
- **They put lot of questions and do not get satisfied with simple answers and are always happy to learn and are curious to know the things.**
- **Such children are innovative and attempt difficult tasks with full concentration to succeed.**
- They are resourceful and stable.

Q. 4. When is the best time to start teaching your child?

Early, **children develop half of their intellectual capacity by age of four and eighty percent by age of six to eight years. Early teaching stimulates better functioning of brain specially structural and chemical wise.**

Q. 5. What should you do to enhance your child's learning/memory?

   a. Look for the situations with one to two years old child as follows just for thirty seconds.

You can either –

- Take the child to window and show him outside.
- Describe the outside features.
- Draw his attention to a particular aspect of outside world.

b.   Or you can identify child's preferred method of learning for building skills.

1.   After identifying – categorize your child as follows.

   i.   The on looker – such children are quiet and prefer solitary activities. They are good at motor skills. They mimic the game after watching. Encourage watching.

   ii.   The listeners – They are social and talkative but poor in motor skills. Teach them motor skills by praising them.

   iii.   The mover – The child is physically and kinesthetically oriented and learn and communicate by sports. Teach them spelling and math skills.

Memory development

Develop child memory by trying following

Try it yourself

Mnemonics – It can help to link something you are trying to remember to an image in your mind, so that when you want to remember it, you have the picture to help you. Another trick is to use a mnemonic. The initial letters of a phrase can be useful for remembering something. For example: "Richard of York gave battle in vain" helps you to remember the colours of the rainbow: red, orange, yellow, green, blue, indigo and violet.

Tray game (Photographic Memory)

Test your memory. Collect some items on a tray. Spend one minute looking at them, then cover the tray with a cloth. How many of the objects can you recall?

2. Use flash cards to present a bit of information.

3. Teach photographic memory – show large of information for few second and ask the child to recall.

4. Teach alphabets – Divide alphabet into three parts, presenting one section at a time for ten seconds, repeat the presentation again and again.

5. Teach the child when he is receptive, not tired or preoccupied, speak with enthusiasm.

6. Allow your child for freedom of activities between two or three choices.

7. Avoid interrupting the child when he is busy in inaction with full concentration. Praise later.

8. End the activity before child feels bored.

9. Connect learning with real life.

10. Make learning a fun. Try game in teaching.

11. Give praise and affection when you stop teaching.

12. Make home atmosphere congenial.

13. Be a firm disciplinarian but affectionate.

14. Spend some quality time with the child.

Q. 6. What makes a child street smart?

Ans. Ability to learn things from life and experience, thus having good judgement on life situation, other people and child himself. The child has to be quick and sensitive to environment.

Q. 7. Who succeeds in life?

A book smart or a street smart. At though education makes a person more powerful and sometimes rich. But knowing society is equally important. In life term, a combination of both is key to success.

Help Your Child to Be an Achiever in Life

Precious gems buried underground need to be mined and polished to become beautiful and shining. Similarly, the jewels of unique potentials possessed by each child need to be discovered and polished to make him shine in life. Good schooling and good academic grades do help them to show some of their potentials. However to bring out other hidden qualities necessary for becoming an outstanding individual of great humanity and profound insight. Following tips may be useful in changing your Child from "can he?" to "HE CAN."

1. Knowledge and Wisdom

2. Good Communication skills

3. Develop good human relationship

4. Positive attitude, confidence and sincerity

5. Smart working

    (a) Effective time management   (b) Way of working

6. Setting goals

7. Learn to challenge difficulties

8. Encouragement, hope and motivation

9. Personality development

10. Friendship – Art of remembering names and faces of people

11. Relaxation (Stress Management)-Following would help in relaxation of a stressed child.

a. Psychotherapy

b. Meditation and Yoga

c. Exercise

d. Avoidance of tension and addictive agents

e. Social activities

f. Good sleep

g. Reading good books

h. Fostering and appreciation for art, culture and nature.

20. 1. Knowledge and wisdom

"Knowledge is Power" – Acquiring knowledge is a gradual process. One has to develop interest in a particular thing to acquire knowledge and also one has to use five senses to keep it intact. The knowledge is acquired through good memory and good concentration. One has to have faith in his/ her memory. We should not call memory as good or bad but it is trained or untrained memory. Through a trained memory we can achieve a better problem solving ability and creative thinking. For memorizing the things, following are important:

i. Timely repetition

ii. Visualize the things in action

iii. Visualize the things illogically

iv. Visualize the things out of proportion

For example if you want to remember the words like garden, doctor, cloud, marriage, horse, aeroplane, hills, stethoscope, trees, flowers. You have to make a story linking these words which may be illogical. You may make a story in a way that a doctor with his stethoscope around his neck is sitting on a big horse back. He is getting married in a garden where there are many trees and hills around. While he was getting married, an aeroplane crossed him showering the flowers. The sky that day was cloudy. The things are being visualized in action and are also out of proportion.

This could be repeated five to seven times and one shall be able to remember the given words. This is how we can train our memory. Concentrate on a subject, ask questions to clear the doubts. This will also train your memory.

Your conscious mind is working only 10–15% while subconscious mind 85–90% which is a store house of memory, hence to train your subconscious mind you have to activate it by the methods just described. Memoirs can also be made to train your memory, taking first letter of each word you want to remember and then combining these first letters to make an understandable word or words or making sentences from each letter.

Give your child good and interesting books to read so that he enjoys reading and not just go to sleep after opening the book. These may be of art, culture, fiction or stories etc. The other way is to associate and link the word with some peculiar/or common object, for example "Fatma" with Fat Amma. Mike with microphone. Ashok with king Ashoka. Memory is information storage system while wisdom is utilizing your brain power in work.

20. 2. Good communication skills

Effective communication generates courage and confidence and also earns more respect and admiration from society. Communication skill basically depends on the personality, self-confidence, knowledge, vocabulary, languages and expression. Parents should let the children speak and reason out. They should listen carefully to their view-point and give honest and sincere appreciation. Make them feel important and confident when they are expressing themselves. Help them to be assertive and not aggressive. Convey to them some of the golden principles of human relations like a smiling face, politeness, respect for others etc.

For good communication skill, one has to have good vocabulary and command on the language. If spoken in a polite way, it wins the hearts of people and gives them confidence about you. Almost half the work is done by your good command of speaking only. Improve vocabulary of the child as much as you can. Record the speech and listen to it again and again. Try to speak in front of mirror, speak again and again, then correct it.

20. 3. Develop good human relationship

Our success in this world is not independent but depends upon mutual benefits. Hence try to develop and maintain relations with every person in personal work and social situations. Following are some rules to be followed:

1. Be a good listener

2. Do not criticize, condemn or complain.

3. Smile

4. Become interested in other people

5. Names are important to remember, calling by name gives a sweetest impact.

6. Sincerely appreciate the person.

20. 4. Positive attitude, confidence and sincerity

1. Make your child responsible.

2. Choose an age appropriate task

3. Set good example as the child imitates his parents.

4. Face the things in a positive way. Give suggestions. Do not bribe the child. Encourage the child for his efforts made for the task. He will improve gradually.

5. Establish the routine

6. Do not condemn the child

7. Never hold parental love

8. Use polite but firm language

The attitude determines the altitude in life. Only those people win who think that "They can." This is our confidence and attitude. Confidence is a psychological booster of our power. Without confidence the person is an engine without spark plugs. **We should act and not react. Keep face values for your actions. Act more decisively and feel calm. It is a tool to make important changes for being successful.**

Be true to yourself and toward others also. If you take up a job, try to finish in that particular period as has been decided. **Maintain the quality, the quantity will automatically come to you. There should always be a sense of commitment.**

20. 5. Smart working

Smart way of working makes the person successful. Following are the ways for smart working:

a) Effective time management: Teach the child to respect the time. This can be taught indirectly by parent's own habit of punctuality. They can help the child to make a time table for himself. Depending upon the age of the child, make him learn the value of time, to be true to himself, to value his own commitments and determination as per the schedule made.

b) Way of working: Most people achieve 20% result after putting 80% efforts but successful people put 20% efforts to achieve 80%. There is an art of working. Always make a list of work you want to do daily or weekly. Try to do most important works first of all, enlist the work which could be postponed for a day or two. Try easier things first and after doing them, put a mark- "done." Try to use letters, phone, fax, 'e-mail if possible, rather than going yourself. If you can take the help of other persons, try to distribute some work to them. This is a smart way of working. Be a smart worker rather than too much hard worker with less of output. Think of getting the work completed. **Hard work is important but not too much hard with less of output.**

20. 6. Setting goals

Help your child to set goals, short term goals and long term goals. To achieve these goals, firstly he has to take care of the tasks at hand seriously and complete them to the best of his abilities, then moving towards the goals with steady and thorough efforts. **Thus the value of hard work, sincerity and commitment remain the key steps.**

20. 7. Learn to challenge difficulties

The children should be given the opportunity to challenge difficulties. May it be in study, play or human relations. Parents don't have to be over protective, instead should be a guide to them. **Don't make them glass children who are physically, emotionally and spiritually weak. Encountering problems, making mistakes and feeling sad about them are most natural. However, important thing is not be defeated by the problems.** Reassure your child, give him the opportunity to be independent. Appreciate the child's work. Ask your child to do the best and leave the rest. Inculcate high esteem (feeling of capability and being loved) in him/her.

20. 8. Encouragement, hope and motivation

A growing child has to face not only the worry and anguish because of his performance and grades in the school but also has to face a variety of problems at home and in school, such as, difficulty in adjustment, worry about his looks, personality, behaviour towards opposite sex and friends. These may lead to a feeling of insecurity, frustration and sometime anxiety or depression. Parents need to understand the problems and give fair advice based on reasoning, giving examples of great people from the history. Child needs encouragement and hope during these moments. The support of the parents would help the child to develop a positive and pro-active attitude in life. This will motivate the child for his future assignments.

20. 9. Personality development

It is difficult to define personality in few lines because it includes many aspects of life and is multifactoral. However, it is not impossible to improve upon ones personality. Gandhiji held the conviction that "we can become anything we want to be." It all depends upon the "strength of determination." Each child is beautiful in its own way, that is, everyone is endowed with his personality to make him an achiever in life. If the positive qualities can be developed over the negative traits, the personality can be improved, for example, if the child is short statured or dark complexioned, never let him feel inferior or worthless, rather help him develop his other qualities which will outshine the negative aspects. **Encourage him by saying "no one's personality is flawless or perfect, no one has only merits or faults." Further the negative emotion in the child, like anger, aggressiveness, unfriendly or intolerant behaviour can be improved by affectionately pointing and suggesting him.** These negative shortcomings will gradually fade and shall no longer be apparent. The positive qualities ultimately radiate.

Parents should not compare the child with other children and also should not bother too much about the opinion of others. It is your child, you have to help him polish, to help him develop his talent. The child will grow more self-confident and happy by developing these creative potentials.

20. 10. Friendship

Help the child to make friends. A German poet Johann Schiller puts it this way **"Friendship doubles ones happiness and reduces ones sadness by half."** Young child's heart is very sensitive, at one moment he may feel everything is great but the next moment suddenly he feels most inadequate and worthless person. Genuine friends at these moments may boost the mood of the child. However, child is to be encouraged to make good friends and maintain the friendship.

They must realize that without genuine friends, the life becomes lonely, unbalanced and self-centered. Parents can guide them by their own example, how much they care about a genuine friendship in their own life. True friendship with persons of outstanding character and ability contributes to one's growth as a person with positive values. Opposite to this, having bad friends will result in insensitive person with negative values. Parents can also help the child to maintain friendship with the colleagues by inculcating certain qualities such as, not to harbour jealousy and be truthful to the relationship. While making friends it is important to remember and calling by name gives a great impact. We often tend to forget the names and faces of the persons after seeing them. The problem is easily remediable. Once you have been introduced to somebody, stop thinking about yourself. Don't become conscious of your dress, face, hair but listen to the name and look at the striking feature of that person:

a. Make a mental impression of all salient features of that person.

b. Repeat the name of the persons as often as possible during conversation with him, eg. Mr. Mathur, where do you live; how many brothers are you Mr. Mathur etc.

c. Associates the new name to something popular as Ashok to king Ashoka. Yasmin to Jasmin flower etc.

20. 11. Relaxation (Stress management)

Relaxation is one of the best method of activating subconscious mind. Relaxation is needed for every human being. In a complicated life, some amount of anxiety is normal to keep the child alert in this world but if it interferes with daily life like sleep, appetite, concentration and routine work, then the child is in stress and needs treatment. The human body has an autonomic nervous system which governs the automatic functions of body. This system consists of sympathetic system which works during stress, fear, fight and flight. The other part is parasympathetic system which works to relax the body. In normal circumstances the two act in parallel. In over-stressed situation, the sympathetic system of the body produces more of a chemical (adrenaline) which causes the heart to beat faster, increase in respiratory rate, trembling of hands, strong desire to pass urine and stool and body aches. Here are some remedial relaxation measures to counter stress.

a. **Psychotherapy** – You may consult a clinical psychotherapist and learn relaxation techniques.

b. **Meditation and yoga** – In yoga "Shavasna" particularly is of help.

c. **Exercise** – Thirty to forty minutes of play or exercise increases body metabolism and circulation. The body produce certain chemicals (endorphins) which counter stress and make body relaxed and calm.

d. **Avoid tension and use of addictive agents** – Lot of tensions could be avoided if proper time management is practiced. Do not leave everything to last minute. Addictive agents like alcohol, use of tobacco and drugs cause brain stimulation/ depression and lead to more of stress situation. These addictives make the child irritable and sleepless.

e. **Social activities** – Social visits and friendship engagements are also important.

f. **Good sleep** – Good sleep goes long way to counter stress. Good sleep means sound sleep for six to eight hours or little more, after which the child feels fresh and restful. Sound sleep is important for relaxation.

g. **Help your child to read good books** – People who have read great writers in their youth, have much richer lives and have broader perspective of life. Reading good books is essential to thinking, for forging character and cultivating one's life. Through such books, the child will ponder, learn and also set his goals in life. Parents can give them good books, help them to select in the library, and encourage good collection at home.

h. **Fostering an appreciation for nature, arts and culture** – Make the children enjoy and appreciate good paintings, music and beauty in nature like plantation. They can be encouraged to learn music, dance, painting or any other creative activity depending upon their age, interest and opportunity. Parents can find good teachers for such purpose.

20. 12. Summary

To summarize, the five basic pillars of success in life are knowledge, communication skills, sincerity, positive attitude and smart working. Knowledge is supposed to contribute 25%. These facts are important for being an achiever in life. Nevertheless, these can be inculcated in children by parents with proper timely care and guidance.

<table><tr><td>**21**</td><td># Raising Your Child's IQ and Making Him Smart</td></tr></table>

Dr. Burton White at Harvard University found that parents can do six things to raise the intelligence level of their child. This was outlined in "The Strong Willed Child" by Dr. Dobson.

1. It is increasingly clear that the origin of human intelligence is formed in a critical period of development between eight and eighteen months of age. The child's experiences during those critical months do more to influence its future intellectual competence that at any time before or after and just six to eight years of life are very important for development of smartness and intelligence in which 80% of intelligence capacity is attained.

2. **The single most important developmental factor in the life of a child is it's mother.** She has more influence on her child's development than any other person or circumstance.

3. The amount of life language directed to a child (not to be confused with television, radio, or overheard conversations) is vital to his development of fundamental linguistic, intellectual and social skills. **The researchers concluded that a rich social life for a 12 to 15-month-old child is the best thing a parent can provide to guarantee a good mind.**

4. Children who are given free access to living areas of their homes progress much faster than those whose movements are restricted.

5. If we are going to produce capable, healthy children, it will be by strengthening family units and by improving the interactions that occur within them.

6. The best parents excel at three key functions:

   - They are superb designers and organizers of their children's environments.

   - They permit-their children to interrupt them for brief 30-second episodes, during which personal consultation, comfort, information, and enthusiasm are exchanged.

- They are-firm disciplinarians while simultaneously showing great affection for their children.

- **A mixture of street smartness and book smartness is required for successful life.**

Books Written by Dr. J.C. Lall & Dr. S.B. Lall

People health series publication

www. childmother. com

1. Pregnancy, Newborn and Growing Child
2. Same in Hindi
3. Parenting – F. A. Q. 1001 questions commonly asked by parents
4. Same as above, in Hindi
5. Allergy
6. Epilepsy
7. Bones, joints and muscle pain
8. Headache
9. Asthma in children
10. Pain abdomen in children
11. Recurrent and persistent cough in children
12. Adolescence
13. Ear, nose and throat problems in children
14. Urinary problems in children
15. Fever in children
16. Short stature
17. Obesity in children
18. Loose motions (Diarrhoea) in children
19. Hindi – Adolescence
20. Raising your child brighter
21. Same as above in Hindi
22. Climate, pollution and you

23. **Common diseases and their treatment**

24. **Health during travelling**

25. **Secret of health – Improve your life style (Live long and stay health)**

26. **Same as above in Hindi**

27. **Seven great health risks (Silent killers)**

28. **Same as above, in Hindi**

29. **Drugs and dosages**

30. **Motivation-Part-1 for younger children**

31. **Same as above, in Hindi**

32. **Motivation Part-2 for adolescents and adults**

33. **Same as above, in Hindi**

34. **Safe motherhood and protection of unborn child**

35. **Same as above, in Hindi**

36. **Normal child**

37. **Effect of pollution on mother and child**

38. **Pediatric diagnosis**

39. **Physical, mental and emotional growth of child as per age – in Hindi**